Babel

Babel

———

Zygmunt Bauman

Ezio Mauro

polity

First published in Italian as *Babel* © Gius. Laterza & Figli. All rights reserved. 2015

This English edition © Polity Press, 2016

Passages from the Italian translated by Nicolò Crisafi

Polity Press
65 Bridge Street
Cambridge CB2 1UR, UK

Polity Press
350 Main Street
Malden, MA 02148, USA

ISBN-13: 978-1-5095-0759-7
ISBN-13: 978-1-5095-0760-3 (pb)

A catalogue record for this book is available from the British Library.

Library of Congress Cataloging-in-Publication Data

Names: Bauman, Zygmunt, 1925- author. | Mauro, Ezio, 1948- author.
Title: Babel / Zygmunt Bauman, Ezio Mauro.
Description: Malden, MA : Polity, 2016. | Includes bibliographical references and index.
Identifiers: LCCN 2015031613| ISBN 9781509507597 (hardback) | ISBN 9781509507603 (paperback) | ISBN 9781509507627 (mobi ebook)
Subjects: LCSH: Social sciences--Philosophy. | State, The. | BISAC: SOCIAL SCIENCE / Sociology / General.
Classification: LCC H61.15 .B38 2016 | DDC 300.1--dc23 LC record available at http://lccn.loc.gov/2015031613

Typeset in 11 on 14 pt Sabon by
Servis Filmsetting Ltd, Stockport, Cheshire
Printed and bound in the UK by CPI Group (UK) Ltd, Croydon

For further information on Polity, visit our website: politybooks.com

Contents

Prologue

'Mine is a dizzying country in which the Lottery is a major element of reality': a place where 'the number of drawings is infinite', 'no decision is final' and 'all branch into others'.

These are Jorge Luis Borges' words, taken from his short story *The Lottery in Babylon*.[1]

The Lottery is an institution that recycles mortal life in an unending string of new beginnings. Each new beginning portends new risks, but in a package deal with new opportunities. None of the beginnings is ultimate and irrevocable. With the Lottery in Babylon, the Greeks invented a way of squeezing the poison out of the sting of that pest, uncertainty. Let us carry on with our reading:

I have known that thing the Greeks knew not – uncertainty. In a chamber of brass, as I faced the strangler's silent scarf, hope did not abandon me; in the river of delights, panic has not failed me. Heraclides Ponticus reports, admiringly, that Pythagoras recalled having been Pyrrhus, and before that,

Euphorbus, and before that, some other mortal; in order to recall similar vicissitudes, I have no need of death, nor even of imposture. I owe that almost monstrous variety to an institution – the Lottery – which is unknown in other nations, or at work in them imperfectly or secretly.

Thanks to the Lottery, many lives can be accommodated in the life of a single mortal. The awesome, harrowing spectre of uncertainty is thereby chased away – or rather re-moulded from a most horrifying liability into a rapturous, elating asset. Instead of more of the same, you opt, by buying a ticket, for the new; and you sign a blank cheque, which is not for you to fill.

It has, as the narrator admits, 'no moral force whatsoever'. It 'appealed not to all a man's faculties, but only to his hopefulness'. The owners of lottery tickets face a two-edged hazard: 'they might win a sum of money or they might be required to pay a fine'. No wonder there were quite a few gutless, mean-spirited Babylonians who preferred to settle for what they already had and to resist the temptation of more wealth – and so steered clear of Lottery offices.

Men who ran the Lottery resorted, however, to a blackmail of sorts: they managed to cause a man who bought none of the Lottery tickets to be widely censured as 'a pusillanimous wretch, a man with no spirit of adventure'. Though they didn't stop at such a half-measure. 'The lottery was made secret, free of charge, and open to all'; most importantly, 'every free man automatically took part in the sacred drawings'. From then on, The Company (running the Lottery) 'with god-like modesty shuns all publicity. Its agents, of course, are secret; the orders it constantly (perhaps continually) imparts are no different from those spread wholesale by impostors.' For all the Babylonians know, or imagine, or surmise, or suspect – 'the Lottery is an interpolation of chance into the order of the universe'. And so, for them it goes without saying that 'to accept errors is to strengthen chance, not contravene it'. True, some 'masked heresiarch' heretics go on whispering that 'the Company has never existed, and never will'; other heretics, though – 'no less despicable' – argue that 'it makes no difference whether one admits or denies the reality of the shadowy corporation, because Babylon is nothing but an infinite game of chance'.

Are we all Babylonians now, whether by design or by default? Gamblers by decree of fate or by our – and our modern ancestors' – past choices ossified into the human condition?

Not exactly. Not only. Let us try to integrate this powerful representation by Borges with a short tale that Aristotle relates in his *Metaphysics*. A man, out of fear of being robbed, hides his treasure in a field. Another one 'digs a hole to plant a tree but instead finds a treasure'. Each man deliberately performs an action aiming for an end that he intends to reach, and yet *chance* intervenes, which, mashing the two actions together, has an outcome that is unexpected, unintended, certainly not looked for.

We may thus complicate Borges' metaphor: even when we do not sign a blank cheque and we do not entrust ourselves to hope, to our decisions, to our actions alone – small or great, private or collective – chance invariably attaches itself to them, with its unforeseen, unexpected, unsought consequences. As Alan Turing pointed out: 'The displacement of a single electron by a billionth of a centimetre at one moment might make the difference between a man being killed by an avalanche a year later, or escaping.'[2]

In the end, between the Babylon imagined by Borges and the world that modernity once promised us – which Jean-Paul Sartre captured in the sublime sentence 'le choix que je suis' ('the choice that I am') – lies the interregnum in which we are living now: a space and a time that are stretched, mobile, immaterial, over which the principle of the heterogeny of ends rules, perhaps, as never before. A disorder which is new, yet still babelic.

Zygmunt Bauman

I

Inside a dematerialized space

Ezio Mauro   Like an invading army in a sleeping kingdom, the crisis, with astonishing ease, marches over the
entire material, institutional and intellectual system of
democratic structures that the West has raised in the
wake of the war: governments, parliaments, intermedi-
ary bodies, social subjects, antagonisms, the welfare
state, parties, and national, international and continen-
tal movements – that is to say, everything that we set up
to develop and perfect the machinery of democracy in
order to protect ourselves in our life together.

We now know that such machinery cannot protect us
on its own, that the crisis penetrates and deforms it as it
marches on, emptying it out. In fact, we are discovering
that swearing by the forms and institutions of democracy does not protect us: it is not enough. Democracy is
not self-sufficient.

We cannot help but wonder, then, to what point the
current crisis will take the changes that it has brought
about. This crisis is economic and financial, if we look
at what triggered it. But it is also political, institutional

---

and, therefore, cultural, if we assess its everyday impact, which can be summed up as follows: democratic government is unstable because everything is out of control.

We all knew right from the start that this would not be a mere blip but a deep transformation, and that the changes that originated in the sphere of financial economy first, then of industry and employment, would soon turn into social and political dynamics whose consequences would affect capitalism and systemic governance as we know them, society's forms of spontaneous organization – in other words, democracy itself.

But what strikes me today is something else, something to which I would like to draw your attention. I shall call it the *autonomy of the crisis*. Let us take a look at it. The crisis is indifferent to the democratic process, it moves under its shadow-line, so to speak, taking advantage of its weaknesses and exaggerating them.

We must therefore acknowledge the fact that the crisis is a force, but one lacking any thinking. This does not mean, of course, that there are no causes, interests, blames and responsibilities in its origin and development, and that there are not those who still reap its benefits to this day. But, as with the wrecking ball that destroys everything at the end of Fellini's *Orchestra Rehearsal*, so it is with the crisis: it is a force that asserts its autonomy without any perceivable theory of itself and its action, without a project, but with a force of action whose consequences are painfully visible.

For this reason, I keep wondering whether my country – and in all likelihood yours too – whether this great Country that is Europe, is able, today, to think itself (if, by 'thinking itself', we mean here reflecting together upon its future, mindful of the past and scanning the horizons in search of some prospect, now that every great Hope has set). As if now, without the ideologies that we have luckily buried behind us, we were no longer able to look together into our hearts and out to what lies ahead. As soon as everything that helped us create this 'together' collapsed – the parties, the great political culture, the modes of expression – the room for thought and discussion suddenly shrank and the current public discourse atrophied. Perhaps we are no longer capable of forming a public opinion, even though we peddle freely in private opinions reduced to pills and pelted around the globe with thousands of daily tweets, and even though we are deep in a sea of comments and shards of judgement spun into jokes, puns, invectives, aphorisms.

You have witnessed the meltdown of everything that was meant to give shape and substance to a solid, well-organized thought that builds up and develops through debate. You gave a name to this phenomenon. Now we have to ask the ultimate, radical question: we must ask whether even the very thought that thinks the liquid world will end up melting. And then we will have to wonder how we will be able to live under the threat of unremitting waves, with no fixed points or instruments to gauge the weight and distance of things, completely alone on the open sea. Because if democracy is under attack – since this is the issue at stake today – we must wonder whether it is still capable of thinking itself, whether it is still capable of re-thinking itself, so as to re-imagine and recover the power to actually govern.

Zygmunt Bauman You hit the bull's-eye when point-ing out that the present crisis, affecting all aspects of our condition, cuts deep into 'everything that we set up to develop and perfect the machinery of democracy in order to protect ourselves in our life together'. Indeed, it does. Suddenly, we all feel vulnerable – singly, severally and all together: as a nation, or indeed as the human species. But, as Thomas Paine warned our ancestors in *Common Sense* (1776), one of the most seminal documents of the modern era:

> when we suffer, or are exposed to the same miseries *by a government,* which we might expect in a country *without government,* our calamity is heightened by reflecting that we furnish the means by which we suffer. Government, like dress, is the badge of lost innocence; the palaces of kings are built on the ruins of the bowers of paradise. For were the impulses of conscience clear, uniform, and irresistibly obeyed, man would need no other lawgiver; but that not being the case, he finds it necessary to surrender up a part of his property to furnish means for the protection of the rest; and this he is induced to do by the same prudence which in every other case advises him out of two evils to choose the least. *Wherefore,* security being the true design and end of government, it unanswerably follows that whatever *form* thereof appears most likely to ensure it to us, with the least experience and greatest benefit, is preferable to all others.[1]

The words above were scribbled down by Paine more than a century after Thomas Hobbes – in his *Leviathan,* another founding document of modernity – proclaimed the assurance and provision of security to be the prime reason, paramount task and inalienable obligation of the state – and hence its *raison d'être.* We can't live without governments properly armed with the means of coercion, Hobbes suggested, because in the absence of such governments people would be afflicted with 'continual fear'; the life of man would then be 'solitary, poor, nasty, brutish, and short'.[2] The purpose of having a government is to be safe. As Sigmund Freud observed, for the sake of greater security we tend to be willing to sacrifice and forfeit a good deal of another value we cherish – that of freedom. Though, as these two values are in practice not fully reconcilable (for every addition to security one must pay with a part of freedom – and vice versa!), human life is doomed to remain a resented but unavoidable compromise between forever incomplete security and forever incomplete freedom. It lies therefore in the nature of that compromise that it can't be fully satisfactory; any specific settlement tempts both sides to try to negotiate or impose a different balance of gains and losses. We move, pendulum-style, from yearning for more freedom to yearning for more security. But we cannot get both of them in sufficient quantity. As English folk wisdom sadly concludes, 'you can't have your cake and eat it too'. As Paine warned us, we are now 'exposed to the same miseries *by a government*, which we might expect in a country *without government*'. That harrowing misery from which we trusted governments to relieve us but that haunts us nowadays on governments' initiative, with governments' active assistance or resigned indifference, is in the nutshell the sense of existential insecurity. As you rightly emphasize, it is by the democratic system as such, that dense network of institutions which our fathers ingeniously designed and laboriously had woven, that a growing number of their successors and our contemporaries feel betrayed and disappointed.

The most gruesome manifestation of that frustration is the distance growing between those who vote and those who are put in power through their vote. Less and less do voters trust the promises made by the people whom they are electing to govern; bitterly disavowed by the broken promises of old, voters hardly expect that this time the promises are likely to be fulfilled. More and more often, voters just go through the motions – guided more by their learned habits than by hopes of a change for the better that their voting will bring. At best, they go to the ballot boxes to choose the lesser between evils. For a large majority of citizens, a prospect of turning the course of events in the right direction – a possibility that used, in the past, to make democracy so attractive and active participation in democratic procedures so desirable – is now seldom, if ever, believed to be on the cards and within reach. As J. M. Coetzee noted in his *Diary of a Bad Year*:

> Faced with a choice between A and B, given the kind of A and the kind of B who usually make it onto the ballot paper, most people, *ordinary* people, are in their hearts inclined to choose neither. But that is only an inclination, and the state does not deal in inclinations. [. . .] The state shakes its head. *You have to choose*, says the state: *A or B.*[3]

We witness these days that traditional choice between 'placid servitude on the one hand and revolt against servitude on the other' falling into disuse, and failing to grasp the present-day attitude taken by most of the electorate towards those whom they elect to govern: a third attitude is fast growing in popularity and is by now 'chosen by thousands of millions of people every day' – a stance described by Coetzee as marked by 'quietism, willed obscurity, or inner emigration'. A breakdown of communication between the political elite and the rest?

Let us bear in mind José Saramago's *Seeing*,[4] that brilliantly insightful 2004 allegory, or rather premonitory intimation – written ten years ago – of where the present gradual though persistent falling of democracy's integrative powers may eventually lead us.

EM You use a word that may well define the whole phase we are living in currently, which will last who knows how long. 'Vulnerable': we the lost individuals are indeed vulnerable, and so is the weakened social structure, and ultimately democracy itself, which is exhausted. This is not merely a political concept but one that is material, physical and psychological at the same time. It shows us how deeply the crisis delves, touching us in the flesh and in the spirit, which our societies have rendered so fragile. And you are right to extend the notion of the crisis, because the economic–financial disorder has been able to spread out of all proportion only insofar as it has found the gates of our democracy already flung wide open and off their hinges, and it was thus able to infiltrate easily the weak spots in the democratic machinery, like rust. The short circuit is clear: perceiving one's vulnerability triggers fear, but if the duty of governments is first and foremost to guarantee security, then the governments become the main suspects in the face of this new, spreading insecurity. In fact, politics ends up being the champion of a world that does not work – its overturned totem.

There is even method in it. The exchange you refer to, which has characterized modernity (I, the citizen, sacrifice quotas of my freedom; you, the state, give me increasing quotas of security, which to me are more valuable) – well, that exchange has stopped. The state has no interest in my quotas because the Stock Market of power does its fixing elsewhere, in the impersonal spaces of financial flows. Most importantly, public power has no certainties and safeguards to offer or trade in, and at any rate it can hardly guarantee what it sells, because government is deteriorating and everything is now out of control.

Originally, however, we had handed over the monopoly of force to the state precisely so that it might defend us as individuals and as a group; we had built, through the free play of politics, a common way to legitimize the political–juridical power and the roles that derive from it. But if that mechanism stops, then the state gives in to the crisis, finance turns out to be an independent variable, labour becomes unstable goods and not a means of setting oneself in relation to others, globalization blows the arena of the crisis out of all proportion, and eventually the role of the citizen and the bonds of mutual dependence that link individuals to public power end up collapsing too.

You identify the breaking point with the widening gap between electors and elected – that is to say, with the evident crisis of representation. People do not vote any more, or they do it with indifference, without passion or at least without much conviction; they do not believe in the right to vote as the most effective way to reward and punish, and to choose. It is true that the problems of representation are ancient and cyclical. Walter Lippmann wrote as early as 1925 that 'the private citizen today has come to feel rather like a deaf spectator in the back row, who ought to keep his mind on the mystery off there, but cannot quite manage to keep awake'.[5] But it is all the more true that this weary, drowsy and puzzled deafness has now paradoxically become a form of reversed politics, as if the disillusion came full circle and the rejection of politics gave shape to 'real anti-politics', just as there once was 'real social-ism'. Jacques Julliard phrases it thus: when the system of representation becomes a 'bad conductor of the general will', at a deeper level the 'rejection of politics reveals the individual's blind aspiration to autonomy, a sort of allergy to the notion of government itself'.[6]

But now, right now, we are one step beyond: the dis-appointed citizen's allergy to government confuses and defies the fundamental concepts of modern political phil-osophy; it spreads from governments and parties to the state and its institutions – until it reaches the final stage, which we have already reached: allergy to democracy itself. We see its signs, from the consensus for Putin's neo-imperialism to the success of Orban or Erdogan. After all, what does that disappointed fundamental need of security amount to, nowadays? Essentially, the fear that democratic governance may not have any form of control, because it cannot manage the crisis and its col-lateral phenomena. We are facing therefore a political instability that is first and foremost a political solitude, a political incommunicability.

I am talking about a new solitude, a new incommuni-cability. In the eyes of power, the traces of information that I leave behind as I live are more important than my actual life and problems (except if I am in the red) which instead interrupt the virtual traces and raise an alarm. Here is the new couple of post-democracy – the state and the citizen – forced to live together without having any reason to, all passion for each other ultimately extinguished. The citizen who, as you say, feels betrayed and frustrated by the democratic promises that the institutional and cultural nets set up by our fathers are not fulfilling (thick nets at that: James Fishkin reckoned that he has elected as many as 101 representatives, from the governor to the sheriff, the senators, the president of the United States, the school council) has no interest in the state, not even in the traditional race for power, because he believes he cannot take part in it, since it feels so distant from him.

He does not feel disappointed, but rather rebellious, the protagonist of a sort of republican secession, almost a new political subject in the counter-politics of rejection. But he does not realize that he too is of no interest to the state, as we were saying, except as a number to account for in the polls, with no face and no history. He does not realize, in other words, that the moment his freedom becomes a private matter and he starts exercising his rights only as an individual, the moment freedom and rights are both unable to coalesce in any sort of project with others, then they become irrelevant and sterile in the eyes of power, since they have lost the ability to set anything in motion. The state knows that I am there statistically, but it also knows that I only count as one and that I have lost the ability to add up with others.

The concept of a public collapses, and it is an unprecedented democratic void, the extent of which we are not yet able to assess. We are missing the element in which an opinion may originate and grow. Perhaps sentiment resists: but more importantly, on closer inspection, what resists is resentment, which truly is the white noise of a defenceless epoch.

Inside a dematerialized space

ZB The incipient modern state's plea for the legitimacy of its claim to authority was the promise of security (as you rightly observe, in all its political, corporeal and psychological meanings); there are reasons to believe that – as Alexis de Tocqueville suggested – the whole 'modern project' was launched in response to the bankruptcy of the *ancien régime*: its ever more glowing and blatant incapability of effective governance and so also the growing sentiment of chaos and uncertainty. One is tempted to characterize that sentiment as an early case of an interregnum – the feeling that the extant modes of acting were no longer working properly while better modes, fit to replace them, were conspicuous by their absence. That was – we may say, with the benefit of hindsight – the first era to experience an overwhelming sense of vulnerability; it simultaneously (and, I am tempted to say, for that very reason) turned into a hothouse in which the seeds of modernity sprouted – or a workshop in which fears were to be recycled into hopes, and hopes into adventurous experiments destined to ossify into the institution of the modern state: that is, a state starkly distinct from its pre-modern predecessor which the great anthropologist Ernest Gellner described as a 'dentistry state', to wit a power engaged in extracting (of added value) by torture, in the form of taxes, homages, spoils of war or downright robbery, but otherwise indifferent to the modes of life the value-producers had practised, or indeed to the ways in which value was produced. The modern state was far more ambitious: it aimed to interfere in every aspect of human life in order to control it – to monitor, to record, to regulate, to administer and to manage aspects of life previously left to life's practitioners to worry about. Building such a state must have appeared to provide the much-needed and desired exit/escape from the condition of an endemic and prospectless vulnerability. The sought-after was a state designed after the pattern of a garden, taking inspiration from the gardener's attitude: replacing wilderness with a pre-designed harmony – an uninhibited chaos of spontaneity with contrived and controlled order. Hence the principle of the state's monopoly to apply force to which you refer (a monopoly akin to the gardener's entitlement to classify plants as welcome or unwelcome, providing the first with growth-favouring sunny, moist and fertile places while exterminating the second). The gardener bears full responsibility for the state of the garden, and so he needs the authority to decide what jobs need to be undertaken and the ability to fulfil his decisions. That principle was at the heart of the modern state's postulate of 'absolute, indivisible sovereignty'. Max Weber memorably moulded that principle into the definition of the state. And the force which the state was to be seen as able to deploy must have been considerable, considering the grandiosity of its ambitions and assumed functions.

The *conditio sine qua non* of the state's monopoly of force was twofold. That monopoly requires that the power (i.e. the ability to have things done) in the hands of the state is large – superior – enough to advantage it in eventual confrontation with powers hostile or detrimental to the order it installs and guards. It also requires that the state-run institutions are endowed with the sole authority to decide to which purposes and targets that superior power is applied. Meeting both conditions assures the state's practical ability to draw the line separating 'power' (deployment of politically endorsed force) from 'violence' (using force lacking political

endorsement). I believe that the presently widespread
ambiance of vulnerability can be traced to the fact that
those conditions are nowadays far from being observed.
The state's 'monopoly of force' is nowadays all but an
illusion, and increasingly viewed as such.

And here, as the Germans say, 'ist der Hund begra-
ben'. A state which has lost its monopoly of force,
and therefore lacks the ability to decide what needs to
done (i.e., what the extant powers need to be used for),
cannot but become (to borrow the felicitous phrase
from Jacques Julliard which you quote) 'a bad conductor of the general will'. All the rest – and surely the
equanimity with which voters perform their citizenship
duty of voting – follows. Indeed – why should you be
excited, worry and care, if whatever you do will be only
remotely, if at all, related to what you would wish to be
done, and will do next to nothing to alleviate the troubles that harrow you and the fears that haunt you? Your
participation and your refusal to participate will have
exactly the same effect – that is, no effect at all on things
that truly matter to you. *Que sera, sera* – whatever I personally and those around me do or desist from doing.
People come and go to and from Palazzi Montecitorio,
Chigi or Madama (the seats of Italian ministries) – but
whoever comes and whoever goes, nothing or next to
nothing changes in your life and prospects. Your future,
and the future of your children, are decided in many
places, more places than you know or know of – but
none of those Palazzi is likely to be listed among them.
So why bother?

Political apathy is not a novelty; it is its present-day
principal causes that are relatively new. Already at the
turn of the nineteenth and twentieth centuries insightful

minds – such as Vilfredo Pareto, Moisey Ostrogorski or Roberto Michels (disciple of Achille Loria) – warned of the passivity of rank-and-file members of political parties, as well as of the great majority of the electorate, caused by the incapacity of ordinary people, equipped with but an average knowledge, to comprehend the awesome complexity of issues which the powers-that-be daily confront and are obliged to tackle. Michels came forward with a concept of the 'iron law of oligarchy': however massive and democratic a political movement might be at the start, it inevitably splits into a small, more or less professional elite and their followers – more or less obedient to their decisions and more or less active in assisting their implementation, but non-participating in the decision-making process for the simple reason of being unable to add to it anything of relevance.

Few if any, however, among the students and observers of political life at that time noted the issue of trust (or rather mistrust) as a cause of political apathy. However politically passive the citizens might have been at the time, the reasons for their settling on the receiving end of politics were not seen to be in their lack of interest or confidence in the capabilities of political parties and the individuals occupying governmental offices or parliamentary seats to influence significantly the shape of things to come; this is why they believed differences between parties and their programmes mattered, and this is why they went to the polling booths. The view prevailing among the observers and opinion-makers of the time was that, precisely because most of the citizens believed in the importance of politics for the quality of their lives, in the power of governments and parliaments 'to make a difference' to the state of society and their own existence, they gladly left to their leaders – believed to possess knowledge and skills they themselves were missing – the job of finding the causes of ills and doing whatever was necessary to remedy whatever was wrong. Their passivity was grounded in trust that governments and parliaments could fulfil that job and – armed as they were with the power and resources it required – deliver on their promises.

This, however, is no longer the case. In our world of planet-wide interdependence and planet-wide circulation of finances, investment capitals, commodities and information, 'fulfilling that job' stays, stubbornly, beyond the grasp and capacity of territorially confined states. The powers that decide the set of options open to any of these states move well beyond the territory subject to its control and severely restrict its space of manoeuvre: decisions taken in the capitals of nation-states bind only inside the state boundaries. A few decades ago, political sovereignty of the territorial state was still believed to be firmly entrenched in its economic, military and cultural autonomies – none of which is nowadays conceivable. Let me quote from *If Mayors Ruled the World* by Benjamin Barber: 'Today, after a long history of regional success, the nation-state is failing us on the global scale. It was the perfect political recipe for the liberty and independence of autonomous peoples and nations. It is utterly unsuited for interdependence.' Today,

> the nation-state is losing its capacity to protect liberty and equality in the face of the scale and complexity of an interdependent world that is outrunning the nationalism and sovereign insularity of its institutions. [. . .] [S]overeignty,

the virtue of the modern nation-state, is beginning to look like a prospective victim of globalization and its daunting scale [. . .] Nation-states cannot address the cross-border challenges of an interdependent world. But neither can they forge institutions across borders that are capable of doing so.[7]

These are, I put to you, the realities of the day, responsible for citizens 'feel[ing] betrayed and frustrated by the democratic promises' – the phenomenon which you so rightly notice; and for territorial governments being increasingly discredited and resented as 'bad conductors of the general will'; and for the growing disenchantment with the legacy of our forefathers: the democratic system enclosed in the boundaries of a sovereign territorial state. But beyond such boundaries, there is no democracy. We have hardly started yet to lay the foundation for building it.

I believe that the chance of salvation for democracy as a preventive medicine for abandonment, alienation, vulnerability and related social ills depends on our ability and resolve to look, think and act above the boundaries of territorial states. Here, alas, there are no short-cuts and instant solutions. We are at the start of a long and tortuous process, neither shorter nor less tortuous than the passage from local communities to the 'imagined community' of the modern nation-states.

EM We live in a period of interregnum, then, and this may help to explain the crisis of governance, of authority, of representation. We are hanging between the 'no longer' and the 'not yet', and thus we are necessarily unstable – nothing around us is fixed, not even our

direction of travel. In fact, there is a lack of any political
movements that helped to undermine the old world and
are now ready to inherit it; there is no ideology identify-
ing a winning vision and spreading it around; there is no
constituent spirit – moral, political, cultural – promising
to give shape to new institutions for the new world.

We are sliding into uncharted territory, and we are
alone in this, out of step, abiding by the forms and
modes that used to regulate our lives and that are now
becoming amorphous as they lose effectiveness and
authority. We are not availing ourselves of politics
anymore, we distrust the institutions that we set up for
ourselves, ultimately we doubt democracy itself, which
seemed the only religion left to us – some thought it was
destined to become universal – after the fall of the false
gods we created in the twentieth century. You recognize
the ultimate reason for all of this: when politics is not
able to weigh on our everyday life, when it does not
respond to our worries about the future of our children,
why do we need it, what is its use-value? But those who
have lost their jobs because of the crisis and at the age
of fifty are not able to find a new one could say the same
about democracy itself: you are not helping me, your
golden rules apply only in times of plenty or they apply
just for those whom they safeguard; we the excluded are
out in the open, cut off from the concrete democratic
process as well as from our rights, since without material freedom there is no political freedom.

Democracy's fate seems to lie in this breach of the
pact between state and citizen, as if it were only an
impermanent human construct, stranded in the last
century and unable to rule the one that has just started:
by definition, democracy does not allow for exceptions

– either it applies to everyone or it will not work. But therein also lies a lesson: after having defeated the dictatorships, democracy does not hold sway forever; it must fight for supremacy every day, in the constant effort to prove its own legitimacy; and politics must go back to dealing with the lives of people in concrete terms, uniting the legitimate interests at stake with the values that democracy holds dear and the ideals that it stands for.

There is indeed a way, then. But we risk missing it, since the interregnum is also a time when the irrationality of decadence is turned loose, in a rebellion motivated more by anguish than by actual freedom; when shamanic figures arise, who reduce the political machinery to their charisma, they appeal to our instincts emotionally, and breed fears to turn them into great trivializations, as if there were such a thing as simple solutions to complex problems. I call this neo-populism, and I believe that it embodies the spirit of our times, a perfect representation of a democratic form progressively emptied out and thus open to all distortions of its content, so that it can be exploited, instead, to funnel all the anger against the system, inciting it for someone else's profit and power-game. The populism of the twenty-first century seems to offer refuge to the little political energy that is left to the exhausted democracies, a last reserve of strength and the illusion of that justice (which is, in fact, a rather summary justice, in the style of a final showdown) that the institutions are afraid they have lost their hold on.

Whether we like it or not, the neo-populism that so fascinates the scattered and disappointed masses seems to be a new way of bringing the citizen back onto the field of public discourse, which is becoming more and more deserted every day. But what 'discourse', and towards what concept of 'public'? Nietzsche warned us that in times of decadence it is easy to lose 'the spontaneous capacity to self-regulate collectively and individually' so that we 'prefer the artificial to the real', letting ' "disinterested" motives' prevail to the point of 'instinctively [choosing] what is harmful'.[8] Rather than public discourse, then, we should be discussing a new system of relations between the leader and the masses, which is coming to the fore in many countries under the banner of the Great Simplification. But if the word 'masses' is entirely inappropriate to define the various solitudes that gather behind those new Pied Pipers – listening to that magic music, as it were, each on their own headphones – even the word 'leader' comes to us from another century and cannot fully account for these changing times. Indeed, the leader nowadays always stands before us as a talented *dilettante* against the professionals of politics, or at least as an outsider, ready to conquer rather than to govern, to rule rather than to represent the institutions that he despises, while the new politicians around him flaunt their ignorance as proof of their authenticity and of the fact that they have nothing to do with the system, a sort of certificate of innocence.

Indeed, you already saw this coming many years ago. Remember? I am quoting from memory: politics is reduced to an event, the guru replaces the leader, notoriety takes the place of fame, and popularity that of reputation. Herein lies the mutation. Politics now lives only in the immediate, in single moments or will-o'-the-wisps, unable as it is to make a theory of itself so as to chart a cultural roadmap. Political gestures, which wear away the moment they are made, take the place of political actions, which may be humble and banal but can influence reality. And so the leader becomes a performer, who no longer tries to be convincing since he merely needs to snatch a daily modicum of consensus and a periodic mandate.

As for us, we are under the illusion that we participate (angrily, even) as we take part in a rally, without realizing that that too has been turned into a show, while consensus is reduced to viewership and citizens to viewers. Politics – or pseudo-politics – and indignation turn on and off like music on a stage and one goes back home as lonely as before, since this relationship is a vertical one, whereas politics and public opinion move horizontally, as they unite us together. What public discourse can arise from this sum of individual secessions that are not able to add up to any form of politics? What collective message? Maybe just the one: will the last person to leave please turn out the lights.

At this point, we must acknowledge the fact that, in the extraordinarily thick web of connections that crisscross our world, we have lost the Ariadne's thread that links individuals to groups, associations to parties and unions, our homes to the lives of others, and all this to politics. Slavoj Žižek puts it even more radically:

> When people claim that everything is open to the media and we no longer have a private life, I claim, on the contrary, that we no longer have a *public* life. What is effectively disappearing here is public life itself, the public sphere proper, in which one operates as a symbolic agent who cannot be reduced to a private individual.[9]

The 'Open sesame!' of our times – that is to say, the mantra of the contemporary world according to which everyone is connected to everyone else, everywhere and anyhow – needs amending: it still holds, except that in the meantime we have lost one important connection, that between private and public. Here we are, in the world of the web, without the thread that may guide us. We too are no longer 'conductors' of that special electricity that has propelled the world through the whole of modernity, changing it and governing it.

Norberto Bobbio understood that anti-politics created the optical illusion of a reserve of strength (which is actually sterile, since it is incapable of translating into institutional play and actual government), and he explained this by saying that politics was invented to allow us to take our time in undoing the knots of the contemporary world, whereas populism promises to cut these knots with a sword. Holding in one's hands the two ends of a severed rope is pointless. The politician who is born out of anti-politics will soon want to be rid of the hindrance of controls and procedures, and will soon start seeing them as a spiderweb that restricts the power of the elected, and limits the splendour of leadership. And when democracy comes to a halt and ceases to have any effect, this impression of leadership and determination may be rewarding and give the illusion that it can offer politics new vitality and efficiency in times when it is going round in circles: the sword that slices through procedures and rules – as if these were not the system of guarantees that we set up for ourselves as we live together.

We live in times when rules are set against a sort of 'nitty-gritty democracy', as if they are the old-age disease of democratism. And you are right in saying that either we learn to inhabit the supranational space politically or we are lost, since that is the space where all decisions are made, not here by us. But there is one problem: the supranational space that is closest to us, the European Union, is seen as a sanctuary for procedures, a collection of rules and parameters with no soul, just an obtuse piece of machinery. It is a paradox: I am convinced that there could already be a European public opinion, discussing the great themes of democracy, freedom and fundamental rights in the West, and thus in Europe too. But the institutions are not able to listen to it, channel it, represent it, and that is why they are always absent in all the crises that open near us, from Gaza to Crimea, Syria, Libya. That is the reason why the citizen feels only the bonds of Europe, not their legitimation. This cannot go on much longer.

ZB The principle on which the arrangement of human cohabitation on the planet, originating about four centuries ago, rests to this very day, despite the profound changes brought about by the widening and deepening interdependence of humanity, is a narrow one, that of the nation-state. As Benjamin Barber opines in the study already quoted: 'Today, after a long history of regional success, the nation-state is failing us on the global scale. It was the perfect political recipe for the liberty and independence of autonomous peoples and nations. It is utterly unsuited for interdependence.' And he suggests: 'The city, always the human habitat of first resort, has in today's globalizing world once again become democracy's best hope.' 'The city', he adds, 'now appears to be our destiny. It is where creativity is unleashed, community solidified, and citizenship realized.' The irreparable defect and weakness of nation-states is that 'too inclined by their nature to rivalry and mutual exclusion, they seem quintessentially indisposed to cooperation and incapable of establishing global common goods'.[10] Whether he is right or wrong remains to be seen. But this is an idea worth thinking about.

Corporate management seems to move away from cooperation, by choking the cooperative flame with the toxic smoke of competition and preventing the cooperative embers from bursting into flame by rendering interpersonal bonds shallow, short-term, prospect-less, frail and unreliable. But cooperation and the instinct of workmanship are born and grow together – and together they die (or rather fall flat or into a coma – they never really die).

Hardly ever do cooperation and craftsmanship happen to be at cross-purposes and in conflict – the craftsman being at his or her best in a society of craftsmen, whereas the society of the 'collaborative commons' is a setting most hospitable to the practice, manifestation and display of craftsmanship. This is the ideal context in which to discover that 'under a thin layer of consumerism lies an ocean of generosity.'[11] This is not to deny the existence in this context of that other human instinct: rivalry. But the kind of rivalry it promotes and sets into play is put to the service of excellence and the gratifying sense of being needed by and useful to others, not of personal appropriation or enrichment. Seen from the perspective of the aggregate, its members' rivalry is in giving or *adding* to the collaborative commons, not in taking and *detracting* from them. And let me recall that, as Peter Sloterdijk insists, referring to Marcel Mauss' classic study of the gift,[12] rather than being a spontaneous outburst of generosity, the giving in question is also felt by the giver as fulfilling an obligation – though an obligation free from grudge and resentment. Exchange of gifts is hardly ever experienced or thought of as an act of self-deprivation or self-sacrifice. In the case of a gift true to its nature, the common opposition between egoism and altruism is effaced. To give means doing good, but also feeling good: the two satisfactions merge into one and are no longer distinguishable from each other.

The natural habitat of the 'culture of giving' was the family and the neighbourhood; the contrived habitat of the 'culture of taking' was the world of business, whose separation from family at the start of the nineteenth century was, according to Max Weber, the birth act of modern capitalism. Yet, in the first, 'solid modern' part of modern capitalism's history, when capitalism lived and thrived off craftsmen turned into hired producers, the industrial plant, one of the most seminal innovations of the capitalist era, tended to be, apart from anything else, a factory of solidarity: its by-product – a staple one – was blending private problems into shared interests. That natural predisposition to blending, consolidating and channelling otherwise diverse and scattered preoccupations into collectively upheld models and postulates of 'good society' supplied fuel to the engine of democracy, targeted on forming/reforming society after the pattern of the family with its 'culture of giving'. Democracy was sustained by continuous translation of private interests into public issues, and public needs into private rights and obligation. With the passage from the society of producers to the society of consumers, the pendulum swung, however, the other way.

Arlie Russell Hochschild notes[13] the essential milestones of that passage, grounding her conclusions in American data – though these are replicated, with minor deviations, in all 'developed' economies. First, with mothers opting for joining the workforce away from home, 'billing customers, stocking shelves, teaching classes and treating patients', while the 'once-available maiden aunts, grandmothers, friends and "give-you-a-hand" neighbours' became increasingly few and far between – if not disappearing from view altogether – family homes turned into frail and unreliable affairs, as well as being emotionally emaciated places. If, in 1900, 'about 10 per cent of marriages ultimately ended in divorce', today 'for first marriages, chances stand at 40 to 50 percent. Those who marry a second or third time are yet more likely to divorce and do so more quickly. Moreover, the percentage of babies born to single mothers reached 40 percent by 2011.' And second, from the 1970s on, 'many people lost confidence that they could hold on to their jobs [. . .]. The long-term contracts once enjoyed by white-collar and union-backed blue-collar workers all but disappeared as companies downsized, merged and restructured. Stable careers, along with pensions and benefits, were increasingly limited to the privileged, with other workers treated as casual labour.' Ironically, 'Manpower Temporary Services' are nowadays among the US' biggest employers. No wonder that workplaces have turned from factories of solidarity into factories of mutual rivalry and suspicion. What will the next round of 'restructuring' and economies bring? Who will be made redundant? It is either him or me. What use is there, therefore, in joining forces? No point in developing loyalty to your workmates, who no longer are comrades-in-arms. No point, either, in developing loyalty to the company. Who knows how long they will allow you to stay? Surely not for long. . .

This is the mentality of our times: it is the mentality

of the society of consumers. The world does not appear to us as an object of our responsibility. Indeed, what sort of responsibility might this be, if whatever we do or abstain from doing has so little, if any, effect on our life prospects? The world appears rather as a huge container for the prospective objects of consumption – and life wisdom dictates a life strategy aimed at taking from that container as much as I can and giving to it as little as I can . . . In his short stretch as British prime minister, John Major worked out and declared the 'Citizen's Charter', which construed the aimed-at 'citizen' as a customer satisfied with the services provided by the state; there was, however, no mention of the citizen being called to participate in shaping state policies, and so also influencing the list of services the state was bound to provide. The good citizen was one who took what the state offered and was glad with what he got.

All this goes to say that the present-date state institutions are conceived, presented and patterned after the model of a market society and its 'culture of taking'. They set a premium on citizens being engrossed in pursuing their own individual interests and abstaining from meddling in public – common to them all – affairs and issues, better left to the undisturbed discretion of professional politicians. The task of governments is to rule, and citizens' abstention from interfering is what they need, desire and promote – even if they don't like to confess to that and resent being told that this is what they are doing. The translation job from private needs to public issues and back – from public needs to private rights and obligation – has been suspended.

You are right: 'we no longer have a public life'. Indeed, the present-day successor of the 'public arena' is populated by private deeds and misdeeds – a sort of a keyhole to spy on whatever goes on in private bedrooms and kitchens. But in the bedrooms and kitchens, as well as in sitting- and guest-rooms shown on TV, or sometimes (though less often) described in the dailies, public issues that insinuate themselves on their contents are noticeable mostly by their absence, and heard by their silence. 'The institutions are not able to listen to [. . .], channel [. . .], represent [public needs]', you observe – again, flawlessly. There is indeed a breakdown in communication between political offices and ordinary people's homes. The yawning gap between the two shows no sign of shrinking. If anything, it seems to be expanding with every step taken by institutions.

And so, each time we try to diagnose the present crisis of democracy, the facts of the matter redirect us to the fast-falling trust in the ability of the extant political institutions to deliver what citizens would demand that they deliver, were they still to believe that the demands would be listened to and taken to heart. But they don't believe it any longer. At least most of them don't, and most of the time. Some vote-catchers, presenting themselves as 'outsiders' untouched by the rot and paralysis 'up there', manage to capitalize on the electorate's frustration and ingratiate themselves with some of its members by making promises that they know – and most people suspect – they won't be able to uphold if elected: promises of short-cuts to sanity and justice, of 'cut[ting] these knots with a sword', as Norberto Bobbio and you graphically put it. As a rule, however, frustration will catch up with them shortly after election. Times of desperation are strewn with the tombs of duplicitous prophets and false saviours.

So where do we land, people worried like you are by the sorry state of democracy and the ever more glaring impotence of the institutions established in its name? With politics reduced to a show, citizens to viewers, political discourse to photo-opportunities, and the battle of ideas to competition between 'spin doctors'?

You say that the grass-roots rebellion is motivated more by anguish than by actual freedom. This sums up well another worry: are there any realistic prospects of a mass movement in defence of our ailing, vulnerable democracy? At the moment, the symptoms are not encouraging. Time and again, people from all walks of life gather in public squares to demonstrate their anguish caused by crumbling existential security and the uncertainty of their and their children's future, sometimes pitch tents and stay in them for a number of days or a few weeks – and then return to their homes, the lucky among them to their workplaces, to the sobering realities of unprepossessing quotidianity and its routines. They know what infuriates them and what they desire to get rid of – but they have only a vague notion, if any, of what they would wish to replace it with. These demonstrations, I am inclined to say, are cases of 'explosive solidarity': for a moment, people suspend the differences in their interests and preferences in order to make the release of accumulated steam, by the very number of protesters, as impressive (and hopefully effective) as possible. But the differences that divide them are suspended only as long as they stop short of debating an alternative model of running things and the shape of the institutions capable of serving it; such a debate would immediately lay bare the depth and width of fissures and rifts that crisscross the apparently, misleadingly united, opposition. This succession of ups and downs repeats itself with awesome regularity – failing, for that reason, to alleviate, let alone cure, the ailments which you describe with such insight and in such detail.

EM   As we converse, an image of what is lacking nowadays comes to mind: the 'roof' – that is to say, something that we share and that may hold us together, giving us a sense of belonging and of our identity in relation to each other. Something that, stretching over us, may define us and give shape to a sense of identitary space. Similarly, the physical roof of the factory that used to keep people within mutual eyesight and earshot, making possible 'the whole' – that shared condition of active citizenship that in turn produces consciousness, roles, rights – collapsed under the pressure of de-localization and automation. It is not by chance, then, that you start off with labour – the beginning of everything – looking at its fragmentation and its reduction to the private exchange of a service for a salary – that is to say, its transformation into a generic commodity. From there on, you widen your scope and grasp the loss of the collective, as soon as labour-as-commodity ceases to work as the social mechanism through which we relate to others, deploy our knowledge, attitudes, abilities and ambitions and build something together, something useful, something 'well done', so that I may produce value while finding fulfilment in my professional skills. This is not just about a product, then, but a whole system of human and social relations, which are thus also cultural and political. We know well the cities that, during the nineteenth and twentieth centuries, seemed to have been built with the same tools that were used in the factories, with the same know-how that later gave rise to political and non-political organizations, and eventually led to parties and trade unions.

Less than a century has gone by and already this world of machinery is overturned – to the point that Jeremy Rifkin is certain that we are walking towards a world without work, due to technological replacement and the robotized automation that is taking man's place. What is at stake here are not just the consequences of such epochal changes in labour, but labour itself. 'Worldwide', writes Rifkin in *The Zero Marginal Cost Society*:

> 25 percent of the adult workforce was either unemployed, underemployed, or discouraged and no longer looking for work in 2011. The International Labor Organization reports that more than 202 million people will be without work in 2013. [. . .] If the current rate of technology displacement in the manufacturing sector continues [. . .] factory employment, which accounted for 163 million jobs in 2003, is likely to be just a few million by 2040, marking the end of mass factory labour in the world.

According to Rifkin, then, 'what we are seeing is the unbundling of productivity from employment. Instead of the former facilitating the latter, it is now eliminating it. But since in capitalist markets capital and labour feed off each other, what happens when so few people are gainfully employed that there are not enough buyers to purchase goods and services from sellers?'[14] One is reminded of Ulrich Beck – with whom you have had the chance to discuss at length – and his alarm for our Western civilization: 'If global capitalism [. . .] dissolves the core values of the work society, a historical link

between capitalism, welfare state and democracy will
break apart', writes Beck in *What is Globalization*:

> Democracy in Europe and North America came into the
> world as 'labour democracy', in the sense that it rested
> upon participation in gainful employment. Citizens had
> to earn their money in one way or another, in order to
> breathe life into political rights and freedoms. Paid labour
> has always underpinned not only private but also politi-
> cal existence. What is at issue today is not 'only' millions
> of unemployed, nor the future of the welfare state, or the
> possibility of greater social justice. Everything we have is
> at stake. Political freedom and democracy in Europe are at
> stake.[15]

It involves us all: 'The Western association of capitalism
with basic political, social and economic rights is not
some "social favour" to be dispensed with when money
gets tight.'

This is the old twentieth-century idea of labour as
a generator of solidarity and as the preferred forum
for allowing private interests to become public issues,
and vice versa. The crisis cut those ties: as you say, it
stripped labour of any overall value. But I shall add that
the crisis did more than that – it had consequences that
we would never have dreamed of. It called into question
some of the rights born with labour, merely on account
of the fact that they have a cost (as all social rights do)
and therefore, in times of economic and financial trouble, they suddenly come to be regarded as dependent
variables that can be cut down. We would never accept
this for other rights: but for workers' rights we do, as if
these were 'dwarf', second-rate rights; as if these were
the only rights to derive from negotiation and struggle,

35

and were therefore subject exclusively to economic compatibilities and demands; as if they were a variable of the economy. And yet the rights that were born from labour and in labour, within the world of production, are part of the daily material democracy from which we all benefit, whether we are employers or employees, because these rights contribute to defining the overall character and quality of our democracy. But as soon as times of crisis come, we are willing to allow the character and quality of our civilization to be tampered with, though invariably at the expense of those who are weaker and less safeguarded.

Once more we find that all are not equal before the crisis; the crisis is not blind or even neutral. Quite the contrary. It is a radical agent, it acts at the edges of the social organism, heightening differences and distances. I mean that the crisis is a political agent that changes our scales of reference and value, the structure of our opinions, our behaviour and even our rights and duties. When you argue that, under the pressure of the crisis, the world moves out of the sphere of our responsibility and our power to intervene – or even only influence events – you show that whether we fight some political battle or lock ourselves in our homes makes no difference for all practical purposes. All this encourages and expands a concept of politics based on pure delegation, in which the citizen exhausts the entire political dimension the moment he casts his vote, with an expression of assent rather than participation – with what one may call a handover (only to grumble and complain in private during the long span between one election and the next, watching from a distance what will become of his individual assent). The 'culture of taking', divorced from all rights–duties of giving and of contributing positively, is not merely a reduction of citizenship relations to a bare minimum: it is actually perfectly instrumental to a populist and charismatic simplification of politics and leadership, or rather a post-modern interpretation of a right-wing tradition, in which the leader is the demiurge who can work out public issues by himself, freeing citizens from the burden of their general civic duties, and leaving them to the solitary sovereignty of their privacy, spurring them to participate not in national political events but in single outbursts of collective emotional reaction, triggered by the oversimplification of love and hate on which populism feeds.

These two worlds are not listening to each other, as you remark. With one difference: the political system seems to have raised the drawbridge, content with just a semblance of participation, transparency and representation, whereas the citizen appears to have lost hold of the lever of change, of connection, of the private's faculty to question the public: the sense of full legitimacy in – that is to say, the right of – asking questions of the political system and demanding answers. Our capacity for opinion is limited, since it has been damaged. We find plenty of reasons to rally and come together to protest, but we can no longer find reasons to build, propose, reform. But in this way politics is reduced to one half, the critical and protesting half – which is useful and in some cases necessary, provided that it develops the other half, so as to turn into hope, responsibility, projects and proposals that are actually able to change things. What we are witnessing, instead, is a sort of 'mystique of change', which constantly evokes change and at the same time postpones it, since the protest does not actually intend to turn into everyday politics, not until the magic day when the Redeemer comes, who will be able to purify the entire system, with which only the impure nowadays meddle. It is not a problem of radicalism, as is by now quite clear: the patterns of behaviour of power are deserving of a much more radical and concrete critique. It is, rather, a problem of otherness, that moves politics to an un-political plane, where it is not by chance that right and left blur, since the traditional categories disappear and the citizen is required to fuel the vote with his anger, which is then preserved in sterilized compartments until the next election season.

But the use of the word 'citizen' here is already inaccurate. The distinction between the public and the crowd, made by scholars such as Robert Ezra Park, still stands: the one is marked by opposition and rational discourse, the other is united by an emotional experience; the former must have 'the ability to think and reason with others', whereas the latter only needs 'the ability to feel and identify'. Having forgotten how to reason with others, we are satisfied with 'emotion', and when we briefly visit the public space, rather than citizens we become 'people'. Or, perhaps, merely 'mass': separate individuals, divided, anonymous, unable to communicate with others and act together – only to react to our needs, without ever forming a shared picture, a collective project.

ZB As you rightly point out, regarding 'the twentieth-century history of labour as a generator of solidarity and as the preferred forum for allowing private interests to become public issues, and vice versa. The crisis cut those ties: as you say, it stripped labour of any overall value' – though I would rather not charge the latest crisis with stripping labour of its value: it only revealed and made conspicuous the fact that labour had been stripped of that value already. It laid bare the situation in which the laboriously built institutions of the modern democratic state lost interest in the management of labour previously viewed and tackled as its paramount function (prerogative, task and obligation). As Jürgen Habermas explained as early as 1973,[16] capitalism was already failing in the performance of that function at the time: part and parcel of its overall and defining function, which was and remains the task of keeping capitalism – a system of buying/selling relationship between capital and labour – going. The elementary condition for successfully performing this function was, according to Habermas, the assurance of a regular encounter between capital willing and resourceful enough to pay the price of labour, and labour in a good enough condition to induce capital to pay it. Under democratic conditions, the price of labour (that is, the cost of reproducing the used-up labour force) transcended, as a rule, capital's ability to pay; hence the progress of democracy had to be – and indeed was – accompanied by the establishment and expansion of social rights in the form institutionalized in the provisions of the welfare state: a considerable part of the costs needed to provide labour fit to be used on the factory floor (such as the costs of good health and proper sanitary conditions, accommodation or education) were to be financed from the state coffers filled with taxpayers' contributions. Habermas spotted quite early the signals of the 'beyond left and right' support for that taxpayer-financed and state-managed reproduction of labour being eroded – and anticipated a 'crisis of legitimation' for the capitalist state. What he couldn't yet envisage in 1973 was the shift of that state from assuring the regular meeting of capital and labour, its paramount function in a society of (mainly industrial) producers, to assuring regular and successful meetings of commodities and clients – its forthcoming paramount function in the future society of consumers: a society that 'interpellates' (Louis Althusser's expression) its members as consumers first, and citizens distant second – and even that on rare carnivalesque occasions. Interpellating state subjects as first and foremost consumers coincides with the state's washing its hands of the obligations undertaken by it in presiding over a society of producers – and hence of the regulatory/administrative tasks once considered its main *raison d'être*, and the responsibilities that ensued.

Well, what we call 'society' – still the largest imagined totality of humans' interconnectedness – is not a solid body resting on similarly tough and inert foundations. Until not so long ago the stage on which human individuals and groups played their roles, 'society' has turned into one of the players. In the 1960s and still in the 1970s, scholarly studies titled 'Organized Society' or 'Administered Society' proliferated. Sociological thought was dominated by Talcott Parsons' vision of the 'social system' as a self-equilibrating, monotonously reproducing entity practising (successfully!) its 'pattern maintenance'. Stability was seen as a 'norm' – and so change was an event calling for explanation by 'abnormal circumstances'; 'social structure' was visualized as primarily a prescribing/proscribing force – a sort of a steel casing, and sometimes a ladder allowing for individual mobility, but otherwise immune to shape-changing pressures; a factor determining human actions, by resisting their impact on itself. It was the anthropologist Victor Turner who suggested the interplay of structure and anti-structure in every known, past and present, society – triggering a long series of studies representing society as a process rather than a structure.

Quite recently, Peter Sloterdijk suggested the co-presence (though in varying measures of varying significance) of two economies – an 'erotic' economy (from 'Eros', the demigod who drives people to seek to fill a lack, appropriation of a previously missing/ lacking object), and a 'thymotic' economy (from Plato's 'thymos' – spiritedness motivated by the need for recognition: humans want other people to acknowledge their presence, they want to feel noted and a part of something important, and resent disregard and neglect; to have one's merits noticed and appreciated is, according to Plato, a fundamental human need). 'The erotic economy', writes Sloterdijk, 'is not just driven by money but by lack. It works through lack and fictions thereof. If there is no lack, it invents it in order to go on': indeed, the 'erotic' or consumerist economy is known to adjust the demand to the offer by tempting prospective customers to desire the products it never thought of 'needing' until exhorted and aroused by another 'hype'.[17] The thymotic economy, on the other hand, 'describes human beings as creatures who want to give instead of take. Thymotic economies understand the human as someone with a deep propensity to give.' He observes however, that 'modern ethics is too erotic and not thymotic enough' – and that changing the balance between them 'would imply a radically changed communal consciousness. This is hard to achieve today, as we are practicing a form of mass culture that destroys such a consciousness through vulgarization and egoism propaganda on a daily basis. There's probably no way around this in consumer societies. Today, the individual is first and foremost a consumer, not a citizen.'

And yet, the thymotic economy was always, and remains, a – perhaps subterranean, but all the same impetuous – current in the society of the consumers. The frequent appeals by the writers of advertising copy to inclinations and impulses at home in the realm of 'thymos' (like 'such a gift will make the person you adore happy' or 'you would be rightly proud, respected and admired for choosing this product') vividly testify to their unextinguished power. The tide of studies showing the expanding size and specific weight of 'commons' – expanses animated with a 'communal spirit' of giving and sharing, cooperation animated by shared causes instead of personal gain and self-promotion – has for some years now been rising continually. And here we return to Brouwer and van Tuinen, who believe that 'under a thin layer of consumerism lies an ocean of generosity'. What the emergent life-philosophy they signal lacks thus far is a political extension, and so also its own significant presence on the political scene – shortfalls that render it less visible than it deserves to be, considering its significance for the prospects of a peaceful and sustainable planet.

Let me quote once more from Coetzee's *Diary of a Bad Year*: 'The question why life must be likened to a race, or why the national economies must race against one another rather than going for a comradely jog together, for the sake of health, is not raised', he observes – only to ask promptly '[why does] the world have to be a kill-or-be-killed gladiatorial amphitheatre rather than, say, a busily cooperative beehive or anthill?'[18]

2

Inside a changing social space

Ezio Mauro It is almost as though the undercurrent of generosity that you see emerging under the pack ice of our time has found no way to express itself. Or at least not in a public form capable of leaving a political mark, of reorganizing structures of value, behaviour and hierarchy. It is unable to turn, as you say, into a philosophy of life, a model, a paradigm, a reference point. One may say that a sum of private generosities – if they do actually exist – does not add up to a collective culture, does not reverse the sign of the times we are living in. We are lacking greater agents able to transform undercurrent into culture, trend into movement, individual gesture into universal meaning. In other words, we are lacking politics. And the spontaneous movements that we are witnessing, these too are far from neutral, they work by breaking apart what they cannot piece back together. A blatant example of this, in my opinion, is the development of the phenomenon of inequality, the new inequalities that that are becoming the trademark of our times. Nobody talks about this any more. And yet these fault lines are tearing our societies apart and – upon closer examination – they carry with them almost all the questions we have raised so far. Of course, inequalities have always existed in our Western societies. But they used to be somehow covered by the sense of 'the whole' that we mentioned and that now no longer exists, or has grown considerably weaker. What are we talking about exactly? The sense of being part of a collective story of unique, free individuals, belonging to different social groups, having various interests and coming from different circumstances, yet still sharing a common vision of development and growth, with shared core values. It is what we call a society. Inequalities used to be tolerated thanks to the offer of a vast array of opportunities. I am referring to universal education, the welfare state, the market for talents, which in many cases managed to compensate imbalances of class, wealth. Even when the weak became aware of such inequalities, they knew nonetheless that they could count on the future of their children, projecting them into better circumstances, investing in a part of that future, increasing their security and their faith in what tomorrow had in store, and thus finding meaning in their commitment to their work and in their role in the complex workings of the machinery of society.

But what were such workings, exactly? First of all, a general trend of growth, the feeling of living in times of disorderly, fragile and maybe even dangerous development, dotted with bubbles of instability: but development nonetheless. Then, the clear and recognizable nature of the various roads to upward social mobility, which were powered by talent, education and by the powerful start of the new forces of technology, with the entire cultural and professional spread that they carried with them. Today those roads are blocked and impassable. All this was probably the last variation of an old socio-political category from past centuries – progress, which kept encouraging us to invest in the future, to think of tomorrow. What we are living nowadays, in contrast, may be read as the end of progress, at least when it is conceived as a unified process. Progresses become plural, and thus each stands on its own; the category breaks into several innovations and regressions that coexist and overlap, without cancelling each other out. And they do this merely by virtue of their separation.

The difference between who is at the top and who falls at the bottom, between those who are safeguarded and those who are expelled is all too noticeable – because this is what we are talking about, the new words capture the new quality of these fault lines. That is why today inequality is the straw that will break the camel's back, disrupting the positive tension that holds society together. Entire chunks of generations, classes, social milieux are sinking in the shipwreck of the crisis, caught between chronic precariousness, which prevents people from fully taking on any new responsibility (such as living one's life freely, buying a house, having children), and expulsion from the world of work, which prevents them from facing up to such responsibilities as they already have towards their family. Here we are: exclusion is the new form of inequality, not just one of its consequences. The world of the excluded grows before our eyes every day – people who are unable to remain in the active society but float at its margins or feel as though they have been expelled, discarded. To them, the doors to a democracy founded on labour and rights are closed, and even when they are open, they are the back entrance that only leads them to the lower floors, without a staircase on to social growth. Worse than that, the use of that staircase is someone else's exclusive prerogative: an instrument of discrimination, a mechanism of privilege. And so the positive tension that keeps society in balance is upset.

What is unprecedented about this is that we are already paying for this exclusion and we live with it every day. If we can keep pretending that the winner and the discarded are still bound by the same social pact, it is also because the social cohesion of our countries still miraculously contains and absorbs these tensions, or at least manages to disperse them. But the excluded actually live on the margins of democracy – they take advantage, materially, only of a small part of it, but otherwise they consider it a foreign, barren, merely rhetorical realm. We are paying for this exclusion because the bonds between the rich and the poor have snapped, and as you have explained in your work, those who live in the cosmopolitan space of financial and informational flows, the space of the elites, no longer feel responsible for those living in the underground of the nation-state, deprived of a professional identity, and thus without a social, political and civic identity either. They no longer feel the need for these bonds or that responsibility; the cultural and economic conditions of our times fully authorize them to carry on by themselves – nobody will hold them accountable for others, who no longer ask anything of them, do not affect them, and consequently are of no interest to them.

Paradoxically, the compassionate conservatism that

does not appreciate the welfare state does envisage a special place for looking after – insufficiently, of course – 'those who have been left behind'. The Left, on the other hand, is no longer able to pronounce the word 'equality', regarding it as old – rather than ancient – as though its sound were empty rhetoric. But actually that sound is simply inauthentic, since it is no longer part of the modern system of beliefs of the Left. Its value has fallen from grace: it has lost all its value. Yet it should be an element of identity for any Left, whatever this word comes to mean, in any epoch. But naturally this repositioning greatly influences the general feeling, the spectrum of public references, since politics is in any case also pedagogy. And so equality has a hard time living outside of politics, outside of social culture, outside of the collective warrant for the right to equality. It still endures in the habits of Christianity, but equality is not a private prayer. And it cannot be satisfied with a few donations to charities or offerings of spare change that may save the soul but do not advance the development of material democracy, the kind that truly safeguards everyone's dignity and freedom. The truth is that a collective destiny has failed us, and indeed the poor no longer scare anyone, since they have no bearing on society, there is no party to represent them, no narrative to make them visible, no class to unite them. The poor are nothing. We sidestep them not just physically, but politically too, since we can do away with them. And that was never the case, before.

I am not even sure that the word 'poor' conveys the stripping of identity that surrounds us and that we are witnesses to. In fact, being 'poor', in our lexicon, still means participating in a social dialectics, even – if only to a small extent – being part of the exchange and the power relations between capital and work. We need, instead, to give a new meaning to something different, that goes beyond this and falls well below, to a parallel dimension, that of the debris from a shipwreck: ex-citizens without further identity, individuals who do not cast any social shadow, do not leave any political trace, right there where we live. It is clear that a new dialectics will soon arise between the excluded and the safeguarded, and it will appear in a new form. But this is the crucial moment, the as-yet-uncertain moment when inequality takes a different shape, different from the social configurations that we used to know. A formless shape, since the excluded are discarded even from our own habits of thought, which reduce them to individual problems able to elicit some compassion, at times, but no longer any kind of sharing. There is no social bond, there can be no sharing, not even from far, extreme distances. There is no 'recognition', as you call it; we receive no signals from that underwater world, we are not able to send signals and we lack the translating tools of politics. And this distance of misrecognition is actually already structuring our vision in a different way, determining our opinions, so that it is now an unconscious form of politics. Vladimir Jankélévitch explains it thus: in the 'pretentious melange of knowledge and ignorance that is misrecognition', preconceived ideas and the lack of curiosity 'numb thought, which starts to grow stagnant' and becomes 'an art of self-justification'.[1] We started off from an undercurrent of generosity, we are now facing the spring of egoism.

Zygmunt Bauman *Jeder stirbt für sich allein*[2] – the 1947 novel by Hans Fallada – leaps to mind right away when you note that nowadays 'a sum of private generosities – if they do actually exist – does not add up to a collective culture', because exactly the same could be said of the unstoppably growing sum of private miseries, the pains suffered by those on the receiving end of the genuine or putative generosity, surely minuscule if measured against the scale of deprivation. Everyone, Fallada would have said, is nowadays alone not only in death, but in the efforts to stay alive. Miseries do not add up; they do not coalesce, and don't gel into a social bond, closed ranks, awareness of shared identity and an articulate and congruous programme. Ours is a society that's crumbled and fallen to pieces – guided by the slogan 'Every man for himself, and the devil take the hindmost'. The abandoned, the excluded – that 'debris from a shipwreck' as you so perceptively label them – do not close ranks. Having been abandoned and excluded, spurned and consigned to the waste, does not beget solidarity: it sires and breeds mutual disrespect, suspicion, spite and loathing – as well as a dogged tug-of-war in the unremitting, all-the-stops-pulled-out strife for the crumbs that fall from the festive tables of consumerist society.

I couldn't agree with you more when you selected the unremittingly rising social inequality in its new incarnation of rejection/exclusion, complete with the public unconcern about its presence in our midst and its contrived invisibility, as 'the trademark of our times' – indeed, as a phenomenon condensing and embodying all that is wrong in our present shared condition. Nor could I agree more with your naming the severance of the bond linking the rich and the poor as its major cause. That severance is indeed the morphological substratum of the new meta-social division, construed by the opposition between mobility and fixity, and underlying all other oppositions and hierarchies – such as between rich and poor, self-asserting and externally determined, controlling and controlled, subjects and objects, and – by the way – between the old and the new strategy and practice of social domination: those using, respectively, coercion by force and rule by contrived uncertainty as their principal tools. The mobility versus fixity division itself is the product of the unilateral termination of the reciprocity of social/economic interdependence that marked the 'solid' phase of capitalist modernity – that between the owners and producers of capital, between the employers and their employees, at a time when the 'fixed' capital invested in heavy, bulky, immovable factory buildings and industrial machinery: in other words, the times of a labour dependent on local capital for its living, matched by the capital dependent on local labour for its profits. In such times, both protagonists, labour and capital, or sellers and buyers of labour, were, so to speak, doomed to durable – perhaps infinite – coexistence, and fated therefore with the inexorable necessity of designing a reciprocally endurable and mutually acceptable *modus co-vivendi* fit to withstand the conflicts of interests and the resulting animosity; keeping local labour (including its currently unemployed 'reserve') in a condition that would allow it to survive the hardships of the factory floor and handle its complex demands was in the interests of – local, immovable, fixed – capital. It is that necessity-dictated unwritten 'compact' that put a natural, unencroachable limit on social inequality. With financial capital taking over from industrial capital as the major mover of distribution of wealth and income, this compact could be – and was – unilaterally cancelled. Mobile, easily transferable, 'the world is my oyster' capital, free to move at any moment to where a greener grass has been spotted, has, however, no interest in the fate and condition of labour fixed to any locality of the planet. While rendering capitals immune to the defensive weapons of locally fixed labour, that circumstance simultaneously disarms and disables those still dependent on capitalist choices for the means of their survival. Against the assaults by fixed capitals on their living standards, workers could fight back with a modicum of success; they are, however, armless when confronting eminently mobile, flickery, capricious, restless and unpredictable 'investors' constantly on the chase of higher profits and ready to fly where fleeting opportunity has been spotted – and the resulting uncertainty built into their existential condition. Trade Unions? Going on strike? Nothing to expect from them, except more factories and offices closed and abandoned by the capital owners offended by the inhospitality, arrogant claims and militancy of the unruly locals.

No wonder that the dismantling of whatever remains of the 'welfare state' (a state dedicated to keeping that encounter regular, repetitive and conducive to buying–selling contracts between capital and labour that are possible and attractive for both sides) has become nowadays as much a 'beyond left and right' matter as its establishment and expansion were previously. It's just like you said: 'the poor no longer scare anyone'. So what else would one expect?!

And finally: 'roads to upward social mobility' have indeed been blocked and made impassable for those told and persuaded to view the inequality ladder as the chance and stimulus for personal advancement and self-assertion. The myths of 'from rags to reaches', 'from being employed to self-employment and from there to employing others', of a straight – even if rough – road to the top open to those keen on hard work and hard swatting, lose their lustre and seductive powers in the face of the massive frustration of college graduates now forced to settle for 'rubbish jobs' instead of the promised plum ones. Add to that the stagnant and all too often falling wages and salaries of those lucky enough to have managed, against awesome adverse odds, to find or to stay in their jobs. 'Progress' no longer augurs a better future: it threatens instead to strip away whatever welfare and security have already been gained.

And this is why I admit that you have – sadly – all the sound reasons for averring that 'the undercurrent of generosity [. . .] emerging under the pack ice of our time has found no way to express itself. Or at least not in a public form capable of leaving a political mark, of reorganizing structures of value, behaviour and hierarchy.' I share your pessimistic view of the present, also of its short-term and possibly even middle-term variety. But I believe that what keeps us living and acting (as opposed to surrendering) is the immortality of hope. And I try as much as I can to hold to Camus' strategic principle, in the practising of which, as I hope, you share: 'I *rebel* – therefore we *exist*!'[3]

EM Yes, but how? I mean, with what language that may be intelligible, with what symbolic gestures that may be visible? The alphabet has broken down, the syntax has fallen apart. In almost all your works, there is this irreducible ground for hope for the disobedient consciousness, the consciousness capable of doing all that is necessary in order to rebel. And I would add: not just for the purposes of wondering, with Colin Crouch, 'how much capitalism can democracy stand?', but in order to carry on raising the question of the relationship between capitalism and democracy, so that the latter, as Thomas Piketty puts it, may 'regain control over' the former, thus reinventing the form of the one and the other.[4]

But if the individual is a citizen who has been stripped of actual citizenship, if he does not feel he is being represented, if the links between his private political solitude and public events have been severed, even rebellion risks being marginal. If power keeps moving around, if it rules here but governs elsewhere, then it becomes unreachable for those who are inevitably constrained to one place, one political landscape, one set of circumstances. Not only that: everything that moves, especially across borders (immigrants, financial capital, globalization, Erasmus, cultural contamination, cosmopolitanism, supranational institutions), frightens and intimidates those who remain where they are, as it appears out of control, without a proper government, and causes one to lose one's sense of direction with regard to place, time, identity.

The only thing that fills the void between 'fixed place' and 'elsewhere' is the dominant vision that underlies both: the elites produce it and reproduce it, they profess it; those who are discarded and excluded may question its consequences, but they do not crack its code, they passively endure it. We already said that exclusion is solitude, and that desperation is personal even though it replicates and multiplies. How can anyone develop an alternative vision by themselves?

The crisis determines a cultural hegemony that we may call the hegemony 'of necessity'. This extends the neoliberal religion beyond its own mistakes, beyond the paradox of its responsibility for the crisis itself, and thus beyond a rational benchmark for measuring cause and effect, costs and benefits. In this sense, it is almost a superstition, which resists the disclosure of reality because it is too strong: or perhaps because actually the other visions are too weak. But this is not all. The hegemony of necessity is based on figures and percentages rather than ideas and theories; it measures everything as a mathematical proportion – it uses financial parameters as the ultimate and definitive indicator.

In this way, such parameters become symbols, they speak for themselves and they require no further justification, they override politics. No, this is the problem: they *are* politics: politics disincarnate, because it manages without people, without culture, without the problem of an electoral judgement, without the competitive challenge of contending subjects, ultimately without ever having to account for anything. Those parameters are the alpha and omega of this Europe, its post-modern Pillars of Hercules. That is why, as we said, we only perceive the bonds of Europe, without knowing where their legitimation lies anymore, and whether such a thing actually exists.

Because numbers, even when they come with the best intentions, cannot take the place of politics, luckily. But also because such parameters, alone, are technically dull almost by necessity, in that they only point to the finishing line but are indifferent to the road and processes that lead up to it. This means that they are indifferent – by definition, or, even better, by nature – to the problem of the consensus with which democratic politics should constantly assess its impact as well as its power, which can never be considered a permanent forfeiture, and must be verified in the aftermath of each victory, because in democracy power is always up for auction. Behind the problem of consensus lie the significant issues of information, knowledge, participation: they are fundamental for the West, if it wants to be consistent with its identitary promises.

So what are we going to do about it? The parameters have expropriated the attributes of politics, reducing it to an instrument and turning one of the surviving ideologies – neo-liberalism – into governmental machinery, even into some sort of material constitution. Contemporary politics has no soul – we know it, it lacks the ability to add something to the legitimate interests that it represents and to marry them with public interest: that 'something' is history, tradition, passion, values and ideals, precisely the things that make flags wave. Yes, but none of this moves the flag of parameters, which dangles inert, as though in Europe it was as windless as on the moon.

It is clear at this stage that I am mainly interested in understanding one thing: the effects of all of this on public opinion. 'Opinion?' one may ask. And also, 'Public?' The fact that we are living under the surface of this cultural hegemony, without any political lever and without any social safety net or point of reference, is visible to the naked eye. It makes it very difficult to put into words a different theory of the crisis, to build a responsible and alternative consciousness, capable of developing, together with others, a new proposal of government and a critique of the current governance. It becomes more and more problematic to reach what Hans-Georg Gadamer calls the 'fusion of horizons',[5] that which forges consciousness, a stance, collective politics and a shared culture out of individual positions, private influences, solitary rebellions.

Opinion is affected by the language of necessity, it dwells deep inside it. It has assimilated the codes of the crisis, and I do not mean merely the figures of yield spread and unemployment, but what they add up to on a metaphysical and moral level: I am afraid that we have now absorbed the decalogue of new faults and modern virtues, the immaterial criminal code that administers responsibilities and penalties and at the same time constructs the new hierarchy of duties, customs, practicalities, what is good, what is better, what is permissible, and consequently all that now sounds wrong.

I am reminded of what John Kenneth Galbraith wrote in 1958:

> A society which sets as its highest goal the production of private consumer good will continue to reflect such attitudes in all its public decisions. It will entrust public decisions to men who regard any other end as incredible – or radical. We have yet to see that not the total of resources but their studied and rational use is the key to achievement.[6]

I read the news of Ken Loach's active support of ECI (European Citizens Initiative) and their effort to collect 1 million signatures to ask for a 'New Deal for

Europe' aimed at financing new projects that might create jobs for young people. Is this a radical gesture? Nowadays, diversity, the smallest departure from conformity, appears to us as radical. But this should rather be the compulsory duty of every reformist left in power, and of every responsible kind of politics, not yet another campaign born on the streets on the margins of politics – because there is nothing left inside, the heart is cold, it beats slower and slower.

You say that, nevertheless, we are the ones holding a very powerful weapon: 'We human beings, equipped with language, with that extraordinary particle – No – that elevates us beyond the evidence of the senses and semblances of truth, cannot refrain from imagining how things may be different from what they are, we cannot be satisfied with what is without going beyond it.' Yes, but where do we carry our 'No' from here, how do we attain the power of movement? Alain Touraine claims that the 'public' is indispensable:

> In the face of the social fragmentation caused by the crisis, power tends to change in its nature, penetrating individuals, their conscience and their behaviour. Precisely insofar as power becomes total, the opposition movement – from which a new social and political life may spring – must move from a total affirmation of the subject and his universal rights, the rights to freedom, to equality and dignity. Specifying that those rights, precisely insofar as they are universal, are above laws and politics.[7]

So, we should be linking the individual and the universal in order to oppose the end of the social, and thus seeking a new foundation in democratic ethics, says Touraine. And you explain well how one can indeed be an opposition. Let us look back at the key image of the rebellion of 1964 in Berkeley, when a student named Mario Savio takes off his shoes, climbs on the roof of a police car in the middle of Sproul Plaza and utters the first words of the speech that will kick-start the rebellion – if everything is a machine:

> [t]here is a time when the operation of the machine becomes so odious, makes you so sick at heart, that you can't take part; you can't even passively take part, and you've got to put your bodies upon the gears and upon the wheels, upon the levers, upon all the apparatus, and you've got to make it stop. And you've got to indicate to the people who run it, to the people who own it, that unless you're free, the machine will be prevented from working at all![8]

A universal speech – don't you think? – that travels across time. And yet there was a loudhailer, a place, a multitude around him, the same multitude that was to give rise to the Free Speech Movement, making students social agents of change around the world. Today only the police car is left. Where is the loudhailer, today, where is the movement, where are the agents? What is the address of the street?

ZB Our conversation thus far has been tremendously rich in sound questions while sorely short on clinching answers. Indeed, question marks dominate our exchange. We start our successive contributions with questions and end them with questions. Each question leads to another. We seek answers, only to find new questions or new approaches to those previously asked and still unanswered. So let me add one more question to that already long and lengthening string of queries – this time a meta-question of sorts: why do we go on asking them, seemingly unable to break out of the vicious circle of puzzles?

I guess that what sets that circle rotating, with little or no prospect of grinding it to a halt, is the sense of an abysmal hiatus separating awareness from capability, design from build, words from deeds, talking from doing – and so, calls from responses and intentions from accomplishments. You hint at the prime, the deepest and perhaps the ultimate cause of this hiatus' refusal to shrink, when you ask 'Where is the loudhailer?' – and the movement, and the agents? And, crucially: 'What is the address of the street?' In other words: who is capable of, and wishing to, make words flesh? Why do those who wish lack the capability to act effectively on their wishes, whereas those who might have such a capability – if there are any – do not wish to use it?

I share fully your concern, and like you I try hard to find the remedy – to crack the mystery of the yawning gap's resistance to being bridged. I have been doing it since a very early stage of my life as a sociologist, which means well above half a century; I have to admit, alas, that thus far my trials have brought no result – while the vision of success drifted steadily farther away instead of coming closer and acquiring clarity. Considering Tony Judt's reminder, 'our disability is discursive',[9] the current plight might indeed look desperate due to the manifest impotence of words. Would knowing 'how to talk about these things' – suggested by Judt as the way out of the current miserable predicament – suffice to invest words with the powers that they either never possessed or so obviously lost, or of which they have been stripped?

Babel

I am far from being alone in having the hopes invested in words, and my efforts to act on those hopes, frustrated. The great José Saramago, a writer to whose insights I am deeply in debt, confessed when turning eighty-six to 'a bitter taste' in his mouth, caused by his certainty 'that the handful of sensible things' he had said in his long life 'turned out after all to be of absolutely no consequence'. That bitterness was the effect of 'the idea of economic democracy [having given] way to a market that is obscenely triumphant [. . .] whilst the idea of a cultural democracy has ended up being replaced by an alienating industrialized mass marketing of culture'; 'people do not choose a government that will bring the market within their control; instead, the market in every way conditions governments to bring the people within its control'. In the result, that market is *not* democratic because the people never elected it and do not govern it, and finally 'because it does not have the people's happiness as its aim'; 'It's not a democracy that we live in, but a plutocracy, which has ceased to be local and close but has become instead at once universal and inaccessible.'[10]

In another of his most recent publications,[11] the already-quoted J. M. Coetzee retells an updated version of Plato's allegory of the cave. One day, one of the cavemen ventured to stagger outdoors. After returning to the cave from his escapade of exploration, he tells his fellows that 'the cave has an outside, and outside the cave it is quite different from inside. There is real life going on out there.' In reply, 'his fellows snigger. You poor fool they say, don't you recognize a dream when you see one? This is what is real (they gesture toward the screen).' The conclusion drawn by Coetzee drips melancholy: 'It is all there in Plato (427–348 BCE), down to the details of the hunched shoulders, the flickering screens, and the myopia.' That ancient allegory of reality and fantasy changing places while aided and abetted by a discursive cover-up, can, alas, be re-read and rewritten in the time of Coetzee's writing with little or no need to change the details of the story of dashed hopes.

You trace the amazing topicality of Plato's story to 'the hegemony of necessity'. But Antonio Gramsci, known to note on 19 December 1929 in his prison letters that he is 'a pessimist because of intelligence, but an optimist because of will', declared as well in a letter to his sister-in-law that he was 'eminently practical': 'My practicality consists in this: in knowing that if you bang your head against the wall, it is your head that will crack and not the wall [. . .]. This is my strength, my only strength.'[12] And he explained that, by 'practicality', he meant that we have to be realistic – brutally honest with ourselves – when it comes to our chances for bringing about change. Only in this way will it be possible to make change in reality, and not just in our wild, wishful dreams. The flipside of this realism, though, is a radical optimism that refuses to admit defeat and insists that change for the better is a real possibility for us. This means it's our job to bring about change; we're not off the hook just because we see how difficult this task is. On the contrary, seeing the task's difficulty is the *beginning* of our work, not the end.

He also unravelled the inborn ambiguity of the proposed strategy with an aphoristic concision and clarity: 'The challenge of modernity is to live without illusions and without becoming disillusioned.'[13] No room left for necessity here. Necessity is an illusion, and worse:

to quote from William Pitt the Younger's speech given in the House of Commons on 18 November 1783, 'necessity is the plea for every infringement of human freedom. It is the argument of tyrants; it is the creed of slaves.'

We are *not* predetermined. Nothing of what we do is inevitable and inescapable, lacking an alternative. Against external pressures clamouring for our obedience and insisting on our surrender, we can rebel – and all too often we do. This, however, does not mean that we are as free to act as we would wish or dream: having done with the bugaboo of *necessity*, we find ourselves confronted face to face by the all-too-real dilemma of *feasibility*. It is the feasibility – or more precisely the accessibility – of our goals, inflected and tempered by the chances of their attainment, that draws the line between realistic and fanciful options and varies the likelihood of alternative individual choices. People choose, but within the limits drawn by the *feasibility of goals* – a factor not open to their choice. 'Being realistic', according to Gramsci, is indeed an ambivalent stance: it enhances the probability of success – but at the price of desisting from the pursuit of other goals, cast off-limits and so beyond reach. Above all, it renders starkly visible the disconcerting complexity of the task – though only to nudge for more effort, not to prompt its abandoning and resignation. Manipulating the odds, the powers-that-be may make some choices exceedingly costly and so reduce their chances of being taken – though they could hardly succeed in the effort to render them impossible to make. The world of humans is a realm of possibilities/probabilities, not determinations and necessities.

The odds are indeed manipulated – and perhaps the

most powerfully and indomitably by what you describe as the dominant vision shared by both the elites who produce, reproduce and profess it – and those 'who are discarded and excluded [who] may question its consequences, but they do not crack its code, they passively endure it'. Gramsci chose for that 'dominant vision' the name of 'hegemonic philosophy', which he saw as permeating and saturating the whole of society from top to bottom, and he insisted that no radical change of society is conceivable unless that philosophy is transformed. The most effective defence against such transformation for the philosophy that is currently hegemonic is its contrived imperceptibility, verging on invisibility, and its awesome capacity to absorb critique and resistance to itself and to recycle them thereby from liabilities into assets. The apparently unassailable holding power of the consumerist culture rests its astonishing success on diverting the roads leading to the acquisition of all and any one of the essential life values (such as dignity, security, social acceptance and recognition, a sense of belonging as well as of distinction, uniqueness and irreplaceability, a meaningful life, pursuit of happiness, self-esteem, or indeed a clear moral conscience) to the shopping malls – shopping having been represented as the universal solution to the most universal of human problems and preoccupations. Once upon a time, all roads led to Rome; now all of them lead through shops.

Quite a few observers blame consumerist culture for one more crime, directly related to the 'crisis of democracy', the focus of our conversation: the crime of transforming the citizen (partly by design, partly by default) into a consumer – that is, into a person expecting services from those who run the country, but neither eager nor invited, or indeed allowed, to participate in its running. This observation is not fanciful: quite a few aspects of contemporary politics seem to confirm it. If that observation is in the final account misleading, it is not because of being untrue, but because it diverts attention from the underlying, crucial causes of the citizens' present-day exodus from the hard responsibilities of politics into the genuine or putative comforts of consumerism – factors of which that exodus is but a consequence. The above observation is faulty because it is 'economic with the truth' – spelling out only one of the great number of factors responsible for the crisis currently besetting the inherited and extant institutions of democracy. That observation omits the hard core of the present trouble: the growing and increasingly manifest impotence of the available instruments of collective political engagement and action, and the resulting vanishing of stakes that, not so long ago, still used to make political involvement so attractive and imperative.

Allow me here to quote from a recent article by Ivan Krastev, a uniquely shrewd observer and analyst of the current ups and downs of political life:

> Some European countries stand today as classic examples of a crisis of democracy brought on by overly low stakes. Why should the Greeks or the Portuguese turn out to vote when they know perfectly well that, in the wake of the troubles associated with the euro, the policies of the next government will be just the same as those of the current one? [. . .] Elections not only are losing their capacity to capture the popular imagination, they are failing to effectively overcome crises. People have begun to lose interest

in them. There is a widespread suspicion that they have become a fool's game.[14]

Well, there is also an equally widespread feeling among electorates that a change of government will change nothing in the condition of the country and their own plight. Governments are known nowadays for either sheltering themselves from responsibility behind the 'laws of the market', 'TINA' ('There Is No Alternative'), and similar forces which they do not control – so promising their electors more, rather than less, hardship; or alternatively making promises on which (as both they themselves and those who put them into office realize only too well) they are incapable of delivering. In most cases, elections replace one irresolute and forceless governing team with another, equally – if not more – crippled and unproductive. Those electors who nevertheless decide to partake of the 'fool's game' are guided primarily by their frustration, caused by the profusion of stillborn promises from the incumbents, rather than by hopes invested in those who aspire to take over. Another quotation from Krastev:

> Unsurprisingly, studies show that the advantages enjoyed by incumbents in Europe are disappearing. Governments are collapsing more quickly than before, and they are being re-elected less often. 'No one is truly elected anymore', the French political thinker Pierre Rosanvallon argues. 'Those in power no longer enjoy the confidence of the voters; they merely reap the benefits of distrust of their opponents and predecessors.[15]

Governments are mistrusted not so much due to the electors' suspicion of incompetence or corruption (though such charges are used by numerous populist fringes as their favoured vote-fishing net), as thanks to the daily spectacle of their ineptitude and ineffectiveness. That in its turn is a product of the notorious bane of all and any government of the day: a chronic deficit of the power that tackling the troubles affecting the daily lives and life prospects of their subjects would demand. Let me take another – lengthy this time, in recognition of its pithiness – quotation from Krastev's illuminating essay:

> Protesting empowers and voting frustrates because capturing the government no longer guarantees that things will change. Elections are losing their central role in democratic politics because citizens no longer believe that their government is actually doing the governing, and also because they do not know whom to blame for their misfortunes. The more transparent our societies become, the more difficult it is for citizens to decide where to direct their anger. We live in a society of 'innocent criminals', where governments prefer to trumpet their impotence rather than their power.
>
> Take the question of rising inequality. If one wants to criticize it, who or what is to be held responsible: The market? The government? New technologies? [. . .] The futile attempts of several leftist governments to raise the taxes paid by the super-rich potently underline the constraints that any government today must face when it comes to economic policy.
>
> Instead of seeking to topple the government, then, should we pity it?[16]

Not for the first time, the amusement conjured by the entertaining clowns in the circus will be mixed with at least a modicum of pity for their unenviable, sorrowful scrapes. Entertainment, I am tempted to say, is. for 'politics as we know it', the last stand. Politicians lean over backwards to offer at least that one gift to their entertainment-hungry electors. What is, by inertia, still called, misleadingly, 'political struggle' is no longer a competition of ideas, but of personalities: the highest scores are garnered by the photogenic, witty and altogether presentable skilful producers of funny one-liners and sound bites. In the unduly neglected prophetic study *Amusing Ourselves to Death*, Neil Postman spotted already in 1985 the prodromal symptoms of the impending end of 'politics as we know it':

> Although the Constitution makes no mention of it, it would appear that fat people are now effectively excluded from running for high political office. Probably bald people as well. Almost certainly those whose looks are not significantly enhanced by the cosmetician's art. Indeed, we may have reached the point where cosmetics has replaced ideology as the field of expertise over which a politician must have competent control.[17]

Postman sketched the future of politics in sombre colours. In times in which stage entertainment sets the obligatory pattern for public behaviour and supplies the prime yardstick by which aspiring and incumbent politicians are evaluated, the era of 'politics as we know it' is bound to grind to a halt. For the whole complex of such departures signalling the coming crisis of politics, Postman blamed culture 'turning into burlesque', in which 'spiritual devastation is more likely to come from an enemy with a smiling face than from one whose countenance exudes suspicion and hate': 'When a population becomes distracted by trivia, when cultural life is redefined as a perpetual round of entertainments, when serious public conversation becomes a form of baby-talk, when, in short, a people become an audience and their public business a vaudeville act, then a nation finds itself at risk.'[18]

No wonder that – as you suggest – 'It becomes more and more problematic to reach what Hans-Georg Gadamer calls the "fusion of horizons".' The Kuwaiti bazaar in which a good chunk – perhaps most – of our life is spent is utterly ill fitted to propagating the fusion of horizons Gadamer had in mind. The sole solidarity of minds and deeds likely to emerge there is that manifested by the peddlers out-shouting each other in extolling the worthiness of their shoddy, second-hand wares.

EM I believe that the cultural hegemony has indeed taken, in our times, the shape of necessity. Let us consider it. Necessity is technically irresponsible, in that it can be passed off as a state of affairs and not as the consequence of given politics; it is universal, in that it looms over us all; it is unimpeachable, in that it comes before politics and economy; it is objective, in that it depends on the crisis; it is elementary, in that it is a container and not a content; lastly, it is self-sufficient, in that it does not require any theorization, it only needs to be stated and proclaimed.

'We are *not* predetermined': this is the loudest battle cry of rebellion that may be uttered nowadays, and it rests on authentic foundations. But the context, social milieu, collective mind, common feeling may indeed be determined. I am not talking of public opinion yet, which I regard as an agent of social action capable of a relative autonomy and potentially open to consciousness – something that moves within a context yet is separate from it, and is at times able to hatch elements of difference, judgement, critique, or maybe even capable of conceiving an idea that can fight against the tide. Rather, I am referring to the spirit of the times, the sentiment of our epoch, the frame of reference for our actions, for our feeling and thinking. This space, too, is not predetermined. But a crucial part of the eternal battle for cultural hegemony is fought here.

Indeed, here takes place what you poignantly call '[m]anipulating the odds', a process that raises from the start the difficulty level of particular courses, pushes certain goals farther and farther away, magnifies specific dangers. Or it may do just the opposite, demeaning opposing ideas and critical concepts, trivializing the theories of diffidence or difference. Trivialization is one of the great registers that power employs in arranging the score of common feeling. The flow of collective feelings can be made to absorb the negative potential of events, which always threatens to be dangerous, by reducing the quality of particular actions and specific occurrences, their dramatic and symbolic character; or by depriving such negative potential of any vitality, handing it back to each citizen individually as an occasional sample of the daily mediocrity surrounding us, a sample which we are to eat up and digest separately, promptly turning our heads to the other side, towards the next form of mediocrity, since a collective and public reflection never really seems worth the effort or the attempt.

As you point out, all this occurs in slight, gradual changes, which are carefully contrived not to raise the tide. Which is to say, more precisely: they are carefully contrived not to give rise to a current of opinion. This is one of the most crucial points in the neo-hegemonic process that you have identified. The entire structure of the perceptive, sensorial, visual, aesthetic and even cultural climate that is to support a widespread common sentiment, must take place outside the cognitive sphere, without even the slightest stimulus to participate, take a stance, show indignation, refusal or consent. And thus, without one ever having to leave one's armchair. Or, even better, without ever leaving one's home. Ideally, by oneself. And, most importantly, without ever being more than a mere spectator.

This is the historic change in perception of our times. Since the new hegemonic machinery cannot cut you out of the processes, it brings you inside, but the seat that has been reserved for you is in the audience. You recognize all the comforts of the times, their sophistication: the lights, the music, the stage, the seats, even the popcorn: but you are merely watching, you can do nothing but watch, and all the while you believe that you are playing a part in the great performance whereas actually you consume only a surrogate of action, with your established role. If you so wish, you can share, applaud, be moved; you are allowed your tears, if need be, and even a reasonable modicum of anger, but always in the confines of your seat, in the dark, and only as the individual reaction of a spectating soul. You then exit, in an orderly fashion.

It is almost tragic to admit, but we are now consumers of that hegemony too. We consume it as we go on with our lives, without recognizing it in its true nature, thus condoning it. You say that the success, or rather the miracle, of modern hegemony lies in its imperceptibility, which verges on invisibility. I would add to this its ability to appear unarmed, so pervasive and yet so seemingly unintentional – and, in particular, free of any ideological character, and therefore more skilled at penetrating every nook and cranny as though it were a neutral element. Precisely, this necessity is accepted as culture, as a superstructure of politics: something that comes before the division of Left and Right, which it does not need and does not even take into consideration because it goes beyond it, exerting an active influence on both worldviews.

We are therefore under the illusion of being not exactly hit, but rather lightly rocked: not by politics, which should indeed stir us up, but by the state of affairs, which rocks us from side to side yet leaves us inert. And who could blame a state of necessity? Who could reasonably fight against a hegemony that nobody proclaims, that has no name, no theory, no banners and emblems? If it has no supporters, it must also have no enemies. It will set in like Saramago's 'blindness', which has no cause and admits of no blame.

The problem is to ascertain the limits of the imperceptibility of this creeping hegemony, which officially makes no sound and has no goals and which acts as though it were not a political creature but the daughter of chaos, the by-product of the crisis, without alternatives. Every action of power always defines its field, and by the same token it always defines the opposite field, that of counter-power. But now we risk overlooking the action, failing to recognize the agent, failing to discern the field: failing to understand the fact that power itself is moving. For the first time, we live in a hegemony that does not appear to have any instigators. It is as though hegemony generated itself, unaware of the consequences and thus fully innocent.

We are therefore the objects of a manipulation that we fail to recognize, completely absorbed as we are in the common sentiment that appears to us to be the 'natural' by-product of this period and not a choice. Objects, victims, spectators: at times we are even satisfied with the representation that we just attended. But it is precisely a representation. We have changed our positions, implicitly accepting a change of roles. We 'receive' politics (the little that is actually being produced); we do not 'make' it. We attend; we do not take part. Therefore we 'bear' political events and the actions of power, without ever taking part in them. You give to these roles a common definition: they are those of consumers. But this has very precise implications, which are even political. Because, naturally, in my passive or collateral role of listener, I believe that I am keeping my good judgement intact, and I do not realize that, on the contrary, this judgement has transformed itself, taking the role of the customer, not of the actor. I can complain, for sure, shout my boos and leave before the end. But, even as I say it, as I do it, I have to face the fact that these rights of mine belong to the spectator, not to the protagonist. Thus, the value of my rights is clearly debased: as a protagonist-citizen I am supposed to have full entitlement to my role, which demands to be exercised and respected; as a spectator, I must remain silent, I must not get anxious, I am allowed to applaud and dissent only during the intervals between the various acts and, for a little longer, at the end.

My status, therefore, is reduced and belittled, while I look at other people's actions instead of actually acting, or I grow stiff in the gestures typical of the spectator, who is sitting at the back, far from the stage. I too become imperceptible, almost invisible. My gestures to the actions of power are instinctive reactions, they are knee-jerk reactions, but they have no effect. I re-act, but my act itself is lost, it goes nowhere. In this way, power manages to do without me, because spectators make up the numbers, but not opinions. Officially, I fall well within the confines of the concept of 'the public' – except that the word in this case no longer means transparent, evident, shared, collective, but takes on different connotations. It means viewership, measured quantitatively rather than qualitatively, as a value that is essentially commercial, no longer political. I remain within flows, fully immersed in the fine dust of information, exposed to the televisionary rites of power. But this machinery goes only in one direction, and all I can do is to change channels or switch the set off when the night comes.

One fundamental issue still remains open. Who decides what I might want to watch, what I might be allowed to witness, to what point I might be able to participate? In other words, who decides the extent of my freedom as a spectator, if this is indeed the role that I am assigned? The logical conclusion of what we have been saying so far is that the cognitive space itself shrinks, and, paradoxically, it does so in the season when accesses, links and connections proliferate. Walter Lippmann writes in his book *Public Opinion* that:

Man is no Aristotelian god contemplating all existence at one glance. He is the creature of an evolution who can just about span a sufficient portion of reality [...] Yet this same creature has invented ways of seeing what no naked eye could see, of hearing what no ear could hear, of weighing immense masses and infinitesimal ones, of counting and separating more items than he can individually remember. He is learning to see with his mind vast portions of the world that he could never see, touch, smell, hear, or remember. Gradually he makes for himself a trustworthy picture inside his head of the world beyond his reach. [. . .] the pictures of themselves, of others, of their needs, purposes, and relationship, are their public opinions. Those pictures which are acted upon by groups of people, or by individuals acting in the name of groups, are Public Opinion with capital letters.[19]

Now, if I am indeed a spectator, I will only react to the images that others are broadcasting, rather than creating my own images. If I am a consumer, someone will provide me with the imaginary content that I am not producing on my own. My field of vision (literal, yes, but mainly metaphorical) – the system of ideas, connections between images, experiences, situations, realities and concepts – shrinks; it is impoverished, and most importantly it grows used to receiving its fuel from the outside. I am no longer able 'to see what no naked eye could see', because this would require a personal elaboration, subjectivity, active participation. I am indebted, I am dependent on images and concepts. I am a customer-citizen: indeed, a consumer. I buy and receive ideas pre-processed and broadcast in forms that are functional to someone else's narrative. I am not required to make any sort of effort in exchange for waiving my right to any form of autonomy. The show comes with its own built-in morals, feelings, judgements. It is the full package, ready to be consumed from start to finish. The results are guaranteed and I cannot change them. I am no longer able to 'see with [the] mind'; I am not required to, therefore it is unnecessary. I am unable to give shape to a worldview. Eventually, I will not even have an image of myself in connection with others. The universe of forms that I am receiving does not allow for unforeseen developments – I can consume it by myself. My final judgement, isolated as it is from any general and public effect and thus from any political value, is not a significant action; it is for my private satisfaction, or to leave a trace on the social networks, and no more. It counts as much as the label of the beer that I have been drinking, in the bottom picture on Facebook.

Connected from head to toe as I am, with all my followers perfectly informed on what channel I am currently watching, with my latest *calembour* ready for Twitter at the end of the episode of *House of Cards*, I feel at the centre of my world – until I discover that, if my vote in the elections counts as nothing (since the political stakes, as you say, are now overly low), a 'like' by the end of my consumer-spectator's day counts even less than that vote, and I do not even know what the stakes are.

ZB 'We are *not* predetermined', you assert – though with a proviso: 'the context, social milieu, collective mind, common feeling may indeed be determined'. Yes indeed! As Karl Marx averred, it is we who make history, but under conditions not of our making. Being-in-the-world means the interplay of continuity and discontinuity, determination and its rupture. Fate (the common name for realities not of our making and choice) sets apart the realistic from the unrealistic, and consequently the likely from the unlikely option – and so the dice of choice are, from the start, loaded, if not crooked. Neither of the two factors can be fully eliminated from the choosing–deciding process: determining powers are never robust and indomitable enough to enjoy immunity to resistance and rejection, and freedom to resist and reject them is never sufficiently disabled and impuissant to render alternative choices inconceivable. Determining powers operate probabilities, not certainties. It is the manipulation of probabilities to which powers-that-be are confined and by which they are bound to measure their efficacy or ineptness.

That said, the fact remains that the probabilities of making alternative choices come to us, human actors, pre-manipulated. Attaching to one choice a high price tag (in whichever – monetary or social – currency) and putting other choices on sale with a huge discount is the simplest, and so also most common – even if not the most effective – way of manipulating the attraction and tempting powers of the options on the shelves. But – as you rightly point out and argue at length – there are other, oblique ways of choice-manipulation, all the more effective for being cleverly camouflaged, disguised as innocuous – with their treacherous intent cryptic, carefully concealed and all but intangible, inaudible and invisible. Resistance to open-faced, *forceful* (not to mention violent) manipulation is what is to be expected – but not an off-hand rejection of *seductive* baits: not, therefore, of (in the words of Joseph S. Nye Jr, former dean of Harvard's Kennedy School of Government) 'soft power', the power of *attraction* – as distinct from the 'hard' (*coercive* and *coercing*) power,[20] but also from the corruptive powers of *bribery*. By use of force, people may be *compelled* to do what they would rather abstain from doing. By use of money (a great deal of money), people may be *induced* to do what, without being bribed, they would not do on their own initiative. By use of seduction, people can be *tempted* to do something for the sheer joy of doing it. The first power counts, and rests its effectiveness, on the human survival (bodily or social) instinct; the second, on human rapacity and avarice; the third, on the human appetite for pleasure. All three types of power may be and are deployed in the manipulation of probabilities of obedience or resistance by subjects to the power-holders' preferences and intentions. But they differ in their convenience, in the risks of adverse reactions, and the costs of application. On all three scores, the third kind of behaviour-manipulating strategy, the 'soft' power of temptation and seduction, beats the other two comfortably and conclusively. The 'soft' power stands out for its unique capability of recycling liabilities into assets: instead of demanding (often forbiddingly high) monetary expenditure, it brings the power-holders lucrative financial profits – indeed, it lubricates the flywheels of our consumerist economy. Indeed, as you say, 'We are therefore the objects of a manipulation that we fail to recognize.' The 'lights, the music, the stage, the seats, even the popcorn' which you list – these and numerous kindred, all avidly sought and gleefully consumed, 'comforts of the times' – are about to replace the creamed-off labour-generated 'added value' in the task of sustaining the 'expanded reproduction' of capital.

'I buy and receive ideas pre-processed and broadcast in forms that are functional to someone else's narrative', you say. Yes, ideas, complete with the evaluation of their propriety and relevance, come to me (or rather are smuggled into and stored in my worldview and toolbox) ready-made: pre-selected and pre-interpreted. This disables me as an author, while simultaneously enabling me as an actor. I know how to proceed, how to act so as not to invite trouble – to avoid censure and the social exclusion likely to follow it. I keep being informed 'in real time' of the latest shifts in the 'talk of the town' and in the rules of 'the only game in town' (the 'cyber-town' – the 'www-town', to be precise). I am – or at least I feel I am – 'on the right track'. This is, to be sure, a pleasurable, comforting feeling: after all, in an environment ruled, monitored and controlled by 'soft power', the dangers of inadvertent non-conformity appear no less awesome and horrifying than they did in Zamiatin's *We* and Orwell's *1984*. In some respects, they seem yet more perilous and alarming: as Ulrich Beck warns in his *Risikogesellschaft*, the risks haunting the denizens of 'late modernity', unlike the old-fashioned dangers of its earlier stages, are not visible to the naked eye. One can't spot them, let alone calculate their volume and gravity, using one's own cognitive tools – eyes, ears, nose, palate and fingers. To note them, and so also to be able to avoid or at least minimize them, one needs the assistance of experts with authority: what is left to the hapless individual with her or his primitive sensual equipment is to trust the experts, people 'in the know'. Deployment of personal critical faculties is ill advised. It is now the experts' responsibility to seek and pinpoint the truth of the matter; our – lay people's – responsibility is confined to following obediently their judgements and recommendations, and keeping on course. Once we have done that, no more responsibility is left for us to carry. You might say that such a division of responsibilities renders us, ordinary folks, not responsible for the state of public – common – affairs; and you would be right to say so.

Being stripped of that responsibility would however be met by most people with relief; they would find that kind of irresponsibility satisfying: comforting, consoling, and all in all reassuring – feeling it to be a case of privilege rather than deprivation. The temptations of irresponsibility are all but irresistible; who among us, mere humans, would – hand on heart – state a preference to carry personally the burden of responsibility for the state and the demeanour of the world? Or even as little as a small share of it? Since the beginning of humanity, humans preferred to leave that responsibility, whole and undivided, to gods and their comfortingly impermeable, impenetrable, unknowable mind and inscrutable intentions. And the languages of so many nations – probably most of them, and perhaps all – contain some equivalent of the proverb 'too much (evil) for one man to cope with': a folk wisdom acquitting its users of the burden of responsibility for the shared world and the duty of interfering with its evils.

The place for people released from responsibility is, as you correctly note, in the audience. For whether the spectacle is entertaining or not, pleasing or not, people in the audience don't feel answerable, and neither assume nor expect they will be charged with liability. It is not quite true that in the audience 'you are merely watching, you can do nothing but watch', as you suggest. People in the stalls or the balcony did not write the play, select the actors or assign the roles; did not direct the performance, set the background music and sound effects, or install the stage lights. It is for that reason that they feel free to *express their emotions* – applaud or hiss and boo – manifesting thereby, simultaneously, the playwright's, actors', director's, composer's and/or

79

engineer's guilt, and their own unblemished innocence. I suppose that, without such insurance, most of the theatre companies most of the evenings would play to empty houses. Let's be frank and honest: most people under most circumstances wouldn't be eager and pleased to put responsibility upon their own shoulders. We don't often line up for our share of liability. Most of us would rather treat responsibility as a hot – repulsively and unbearably hot – potato. This is the truth, however sad it might sound.

In a recent book titled in the French original *Petite Poucette* and in its English translation *Thumbelina*,[21] Michel Serres suggests that, 'without us even realizing it, a new kind of human being was born in the brief period of time that separates us from the 1970s'. Serres proposes a long list of profound differences that at present separate adults from the young. Formatted as they tend to be by the media and by advertising much more than by whatever remains of the schools of thousands years ago – which Serres compares to 'stars whose light we receive, but which astrophysics calculates have been dead a long time' – the young of today live in a 'connectivity' that has stealthily replaced the old-time collectivities. They act under a presumption of competence, instead of that of incompetence in need of education conducted in 'institutional frameworks that come from a time they no longer recognize'. The young of today 'have access to all people' with their smartphones. With Global Positioning Systems, they have access 'to all places. With the Internet, to all knowledge'. The place of honour (or dishonour, depending on your axiological stance) in his inventory of watershed changes whose consequences, in his opinion, we are only beginning to notice, and have not as yet started to study in earnest, Serres reserves for the 'unravelling' of belonging: 'Everyone speaks of the death of ideologies, but what is disappearing is rather the *belongings* recruited by those ideologies. [. . .] We adults have not invented any new social links; our generalized tendency toward suspicion, critique, and indignation had led instead to their destruction.'

The aura painted in Serres' study augurs a profound change in the human condition and mode of life, perhaps unprecedented in its radicalism and comprehensiveness – but a change occurring without ideologies, massive political movements, planning offices, *politburos* and general staffs: not a planned, designed, monitored, administered and controlled change, but a change emerging by its own logic and momentum from diffuse, dispersed, poorly coordinated acts of diffuse, dispersed, poorly coordinated actors – a change akin more to natural evolution than to a managed and supervised process. With inter-human bonds fast dissolving, with rising fluidity of belonging and its unavoidable outcome – the jarring and stubborn absence of a collective agent capable of gelling into a collective subject of sustained action – the impending change is being brought about by masses of interconnected loners: by solitary agents constantly in touch. What is presently happening, what we currently witness, and to whose peculiarity we need to adjust by weaving anew the conceptual nets in which we attempt to grasp our socio-political–economic–psychical realities, is not just a new turn in history, but a novel way in which history is being made.

3

Interconnected loners

Ezio Mauro   We have come to a knot. All the threads that we have been following so far lead us to the issue of responsibility. I would say that the range of offer to which we are accustomed may insidiously tempt us to shed our responsibilities. In the age of Google and Wikipedia, we look to technology not just for a solution, but – often without realizing it – for a selection. What we are leaving out of our cognitive process is precisely selection: that is to say, the ability to study, understand, discard, define, refine and eventually choose. Indeed, this unburdening is exactly what makes technology so seductive and wonderful. We do not even see the process anymore, we do not see the concept, blinded as we are by the swiftness of the solution. But in this short space of the invisible – and blessed – swiftness of selection, in fact, there goes a piece of our responsibility or at least of its mechanism, which consists in the ability to analyse, the intelligence to discern, the will to opt for a specific choice. There goes, then, a piece of the structure that gives shape to public opinion.

Interconnected loners

You say that today we experience responsibility as a burden, since it carries with it an obligation to make choices, to judge and take a stance. And yet responsibility was once a concept of modernity: mankind had become fully masters of their own choices and could therefore be held accountable without any filters or deceptions. In this sense, responsibility implies the subjects' rights as well as their obligations to others, and therefore it is one of the various guarantees that we go about exchanging in our relational life. And by granting and expecting responsibility, we all the while set a limit to power and acknowledge it. It is not by chance that, during the Lewinsky scandal, Bill Clinton admitted that without responsibility power could easily become abuse. 'I did it for the worst possible reason', admitted the US president: 'just because I could'. This is a revelation of the nakedness of power, which becomes self-referential the moment the responsibilities of politics start to fail.

You overturn the outcomes, because the obligations themselves have been overturned: without a duty to select and decide, the citizen is truly a spectator, perfectly free, finally 'innocent', in that he is not bound to causes or accountable for consequences. Feeling no responsibility means two things: not demanding any subjectivity, and not recognizing any bonds. Probably, this is a new way for today's human beings to feel free, the restricted sphere of contemporary freedom: not in the fullness of one's powers, then, when one's rights are all fully active – but, on the contrary, free insofar as one has been freed, voided of sociality and its codes, unencumbered of the obligations and burdens of duties and engagements, alone in the connectivity and with

83

no collectivity, as you say, quoting Serres; cleared even of the feeble bonds that constituted the old sense of belonging.

Much, if not everything, holds up. It makes me think that this new kind of human being is very vulnerable to manipulation, to orders perhaps, probably to a consensus without an agreement: cold and occasional, diffident and gregarious, the incarnation of a pale version of politics that is as low-frequency as the current one, which seems no different from mere administration. Thus, disengaged from the social or moral – and therefore political – bonds of responsibility, carried on the calm high seas of a new passive innocence, the citizen becomes the ideal subject for the 'soft power' that you talk about, which cleverly exploits seduction instead of strength so as to rig the game of probabilities by directing events towards the outcomes that it has in mind. It is capable of building consensus by a path that is seemingly autonomous and theoretically free, but has actually been manipulated emotionally.

If this is indeed 'the new kind of human being' created by the transformations of the last forty years, one may call it disempowered with respect to the faculties and potential to which we were accustomed. But when did this happen, in what time and how far back from today? And compared to what models? Would twentieth-century man really be more suited to navigate the connectivity without complexity in which we are immersed? Can we be sure of that? I believe that he would be better able to defend himself, living his times more critically: this is for sure. But the ideal product of the new times is not this man. Probably, over the course of these years, the progressive rarefaction of the public sphere has gone hand in hand with the concentration of the private sphere as the domain where all the great open issues are precipitated and fragmented as personal problems that everyone faces and solves – if they are lucky – on their own. This change of domain has tipped the scales of gratifications, securities and fears; it has changed spheres and redefined spaces and obligations, and thus roles.

The man who lived through this process from the seventies to this day has chosen self-refinement or obtuseness according to the opportunities and risks he was met with; he has made choices and modelled himself after the social demands or possibilities that were available to him, until he has eventually become the 'interconnected loner' that you mentioned.

An expert in the relationship between communication and power, Manuel Castells, puts the same issue in different terms: a chunk of our active presence on the web is closer to 'electronic autism' than to actual communication. In fact, the new way to communicate on the web is certainly mass communication, in that it is potentially directed to a global audience, but 'At the same time, it is self-communication because the production of the message is self-generated, the definition of the potential receiver(s) is self-directed, and the retrieval of specific messages or content from the World Wide Web and electronic networks is self-selected.'[1] Castells calls 'mass self-communication'[2] this historically new form of communication that has transformed television (the new generation has cut off the 'unified remote control' – that is to say, the show schedule predetermined by the broadcaster, which has now been replaced by an on-demand approach that takes from the web the content that the web itself recommends), and turned newspapers into webified organizations.

The professional mediator, whom you previously called 'the expert', has been cut out. If I can do it all by myself, every form of mediation is unwarranted and arrogant: if I can cut this out, there will be an improvement in directness and speed, two commandments of the web. If I can ask the web, directly, I do not want any mediators. The accumulation of experience that becomes knowledge, the ordered development that becomes science – or at least a well-established wisdom – has less appeal than the instantaneous and instinctive message of a casual witness to events. Indeed, precisely insofar as they are casual and improvised, message and messenger lack a specific professional expertise, therefore they do not come with the caste or corporative associations that such expertise generally involves. What is merely naïve is seen as spontaneous, as lying outside of the traditional canon: it sounds more authentic, virgin and capable of receiving the direct imprint of what it witnesses without the filters of the trade.

It is Being (I should say 'Being-there') that prevails over Becoming, as Castells again points out.

But, naturally, along with mediation, organization is cut out too. Professional information, in fact, does not reproduce an event mechanically, but recreates it, reworking it in a wider context that frames it, gives it a new order and helps to explain it. This organization that reworks the facts, ordering them in a coherent and intelligent hierarchy, is an essential part of knowledge. But, first and foremost, it is an essential part of information itself. Yet now it seems as if the new 'mass self-communication' could do without it, could even bypass the whole thing, discarding it. But this is the inevitable consequence of the invention of a web-time that exceeds biological time, the social time regulated by Taylorism, and has then become what Castells calls 'timeless time, which is the time of the short "now" with no sequence or cycle', a web-time that 'has no past and no future [. . .] It is the cancellation of sequence, thus of time.'[3] Indeed,

> the relationship to time is defined by the use of information and communication technologies in a relentless effort to annihilate time by negating sequencing: on [the] one hand, by compressing time (as in split-second global financial transactions or the generalized practice of multitasking, squeezing more activity into a given); on the other hand, by blurring the sequence of social practices, including past, present, and future in a random order, like in the electronic hypertext of Web 2.0 or the blurring of life-cycle patterns in both work and parenting.[4]

It is clear that in this new relationship to time, what we have built with time and owes its existence to time gets lost: for example, experience, competence, knowledge. If everything is simultaneous, only what is immediate counts, not what has been accumulated, and even memory is only spent as nostalgia to be experienced once more, a vintage to buy and consume, not a point of reference or discussion.

It is also clear that all this has important consequences for the creation of a consciousness of reality that goes beyond oneself and the palpable perimeter of one's direct experience. Its consequences or one's faculty to judge what happens are significant, especially if they extend outside of that perimeter. Can a public opinion that is outside of time ever exist, a public opinion which only has the 'here and now' as its inevitable and limited domain?

Here and now, impression takes the place of opinion. In other words, it becomes something that is received, but not reworked, because there is no time and it is not organized, because there is no way.

An intuition, reality leaving its mark, yes, but out of context and out of a frame. Judgement becomes a sensation. An immediate one, even. But it is not challenging, not durable, not constitutive of a cultural identity, of a position one can refer to. Judgement is a process; a sensation is a moment. Judgement is mine, autonomous, chosen; a sensation is almost involuntary, uncontrolled. As for public opinion: a cluster of individual impressions, an incoherent sum of personal sensations, is not enough to give it a shape.

We said that we are without a 'public': we now find out that we are also without an opinion.

Zygmunt Bauman You write: 'we look to technology not just for a solution, but – often without realizing it – for a selection'. Yes, indeed – many of us most of the time, and all of us at least on some occasions, crave and grope for some clarity in the irritatingly opaque, and some logic in the annoyingly unintelligible, world – some lucid tune in the confusingly hurly-burly, cacophonic noise; some understanding, which Ludwig Wittgenstein unpacked as the knowledge how to go on. Almost 100 years ago, at a very early stage in the still-brief history of that 'mass self-communication' or 'electronic autism' of Castells, and well before the advent of the laptop, tablet and smartphone era, Paul

Lazarsfeld found a similar craving in readers of dailies
and listeners to radio – and recorded the role played by
'local opinion leaders' in relieving them of confusion
and keeping them afloat: at a time when human communication was mostly, almost exclusively, face to face,
conducted among neighbours rather than anonymous
Twitter-senders of messages blinking on screens, and
spiritual proximity and physical proximity almost overlapped, those local opinion leaders pre-selected the true
from the false and the relevant from the immaterial for
the use of those adrift – disoriented and perplexed. I
wonder whether Lazarsfeld would have received similar results were he to repeat his research today. He
conducted his study well before communities came to
be supplanted by 'networks' – forms of association
made to the measure of 'self-communication'. In stark
opposition to the old-style communities, a network is a
grouping (more correctly, a list or a roll-call of names or
addresses) meant to be selected/composed by the individual on his/her sole responsibility for the selection of
links and nods. Its 'membership' and boundaries are not
'given'; neither are they fixed – they are friable and eminently pliable; defined, drawn and endlessly redefined
and re-drawn at will by the network's composer placed
firmly in its centre. By origin and by its mode of existence, it is but an extension of the self, or a carapace with
which the ego surrounds itself for its own safety: cutting
its own, hopefully secure, niche out of the dumbfound-
ing, inhospitable and perhaps – who knows?! – hostile
offline world. A 'network' is not a space for challenges
to the received ideas and preferences of its creator – it
is rather an extended replica or magnifying mirror of its
weaver, populated solely by like-minded people, saying

what the person who admitted them is willing to hear, and ready to applaud whatever the person who admitted or appointed them says; dissenters, individuals holding to contrary – or just unfamiliar and thus uncomfortably puzzling – opinions are exiled (or, at least consolingly, amenable to being banished) at the first sign of their discordance. As there are no 'opinion leaders' there offering release from responsibility for the verdict, many a network-dissenter opts for the safety brought and sustained by similarity – nay, identity – of views and attitudes, eliminating in advance the chances of dissent, confrontation, friction and clashes. The collateral casualty of opting for such safety is, however – inevitably – the loss of that 'ability to analyse, the intelligence to discern' whose absence you so rightly bewail, considering how crucial they are for genuine liberty.

A network is an electronic replica of the bricks-and-mortar 'gated community', fenced off from the 'world out there' – a world that, due to the erosion of, or losing or failing to learn, the skills needed to move through it (let alone to live in it), becomes too frightening for venturing a voyage of discovery – as it became for Plato's cavemen. A network all too easily turns into a cage with a lock without a keyhole, and with all four of Francis Bacon's idols (of tribe, cave, marketplace and theatre) guarding the exit – yet more efficacious and indomitable for the absence of competition. If the present-day variety of Plato's cavemen don't mind being so incarcerated, it is because they have been stripped of the will to venture out, or never managed to learn its purpose. As we know from the experience of long-term prisoners, the day of their release into the pandemonium of the world outside the prison walls is full of shocks and traumatic.

And let me add that, in guarding the exit (though not the entry), the modern caveman has acquired a powerful ally whom Plato did not, and could not, presage: the Internet providers, with Google clearly well ahead of the pack and dwarfing all running behind. There is big marketing money ready to support Google in the designing and application of the cutting-edge technology of 'audience (and/or clientele) targeting'. That technology is uniquely dexterous and quick at spotting the pattern of your preferences of which even you yourself might have been blissfully unaware – also the criteria by which you've picked up human nodes when sewing your network; and, having done this, that technology will take care of gratifying – without your begging and no-questions-asked – your conscious or unconscious drive for the company of the like-minded. It will take care of bringing them to your attention and keeping them there while keeping out of bounds all those who could annoy and unnerve you through ruffling the self-contented ataraxia of your comfort zone. Sealing off the access of competition as hermetically as possible makes good business sense – for peddlers of ideologies and of consumer commodities alike.

Another – even if closely connected – point: you quote Bill Clinton's blunt admission, 'I did it for the worst possible reason: just because I could.' One would wish more politicians of importance would similarly gather the courage that this kind of admission requires, and be equally clear-minded in knowing that they should. Because nowadays this is the most common cause of options being selected, decisions made and steps taken. Max Weber memorably defined 'instrumental rationality' as the attitude guiding the conduct of modern men and women. Instrumental rationality assumes a purposeful action, selection of purpose preceding the search and choice of the most effective and efficient means. In fact, however, the opposite sequence is nowadays all too often in operation. It is 'the worst possible reason', as Clinton called it – a 'we can do it, so we will do it' reasoning – that tends to guide most of our action. Pharmaceutical companies are busy inventing pathological conditions – new diseases, new discomforts, new threats and new fears of threats – that might require the compounds their laboratories have just put together or come across by accident, whereas military strategists, aided and abetted by their political bosses, seek targets on which the warehouses overfilled with the latest products of the weapons industry can be unloaded. The art of marketing, the fly-wheel of the consumer-guided economy, is focused on recycling offers into demand by hammering home the principle 'now you *can* have it, so you *must* buy it. You must acquire it and show that you have – as must everybody who wants to be somebody.' We are aware now – after the damage has been done – that a tremendous lot of inhuman atrocities were committed and a lot of human suffering caused in the past by the Machiavellian axiom that 'the end justifies the means'. We are yet to calculate, however, the harm already perpetrated, as well as the damage likely to be yet inflicted, by the reversal of that deplorable assumption – 'the means justify the ends': a reversal no less calamitous than the assumption it reversed – and pregnant with consequences no less grievous and lamentable than the previously mentioned disablement and incapacitation perpetrated by the time spent in the contrived homogeneity of the online 'comfort-zone' shelter.

Yet it is a shelter so unfit for acquiring and honing the skills needed to deal with the harsh realities of the heterogeneous offline existence, filled as it is, and must be, with clashes of interests, confrontations between all-too-often incompatible values, preferences and ideals as well as inter-communal miscomprehensions and strife, and yearning therefore for the skills and practices of genuine dialogue, as distinct from the all-too-common pseudo-dialogue: in fact a monologue conducted in a tightly insulated echo chamber.

EM The modern apple that the serpent is offering us is precisely this: a solution that overrides any decision and absorbs it, since it already includes it. The mechanism according to which 'if I can do it, I will do it' actually still involves some small and feeble reserve of responsibility: I am the one who decides, even if, as I quickly go down the slide, I can only catch a glimpse of the pre-solved outcomes before I manage to see any of the potential problems and political, moral and relational implications. But there is one additional step: the mediation of technology, and therefore of modernity and of its inherent seductiveness, its prestige. You are not the one who decides that you can do it. It is only the authority of a third party – technology – that, digging into the future, is able to predict it and govern it; it anticipates, moulds and crossbreeds it with your necessities and aspirations, it transforms the whole into objects and products that are aesthetically capable of giving shape to the times we live in, and, most importantly, it functions as a safeguard.

It is as though technology has turned into culture itself, or even into politics. Technology operates in the current disorientation as though it knew where it was going; at any rate, it knows how to get there and, most importantly, how to guide us there, and at every stage, at every turn, it validates us and itself: it was possible to get here – it tells us – therefore it was right to do so. Even better: tomorrow will be like this, it is inevitable, so we might as well anticipate it – I can vouchsafe for it. It is a new autonomous morality that has nothing to do with the debate on the significance of the limits of science, but rather concerns the mandate we give to technology, which at the moment is such that it invalidates all questions while we are busy looking for answers. Indeed, it is as though we thought: if science can do it, then it is right to do it. If technology has done it, then progress asks us to do it. I am again relieved of my responsibility, and at the same time I am once and for all authorized to be so. Everything happens outside of me.

The new surveillance system of the National Security Agency (NSA) is not happy just to suck our data from the submarine cables through which all information transits. 'If it can' spy on the delegates at the London G20, why should it not do so? 'If it can' work on the guest registers of 350 hotels across the globe, why should it refrain from it? 'If it can' deduce, from one's videogame-playing habits, leadership skills, strategic inclinations, *esprit de corps*, why should it relinquish them? In this case, power celebrates its irresponsible innocence simply by sitting in the slipstream of science: I am technically capable of looking into your life, into its every nook and cranny, for your security and everyone else's. Therefore I do it. And if, in order to do this, I must operate incognito, beyond any checks, without you knowing, so be it: I will certainly take advantage of this prerogative. The system of mandates finds its own progressive self-legitimation and self-justification, as it expands to the extent that it slips from science into politics.

If what is technically possible is also legitimate, then what is effective becomes appropriate – and it does not matter whether it is legal or not. Long-distance action, made possible by new technology (which moves capitals, but also keeps people under surveillance or hits military objectives with a drone-strike), creates a gap between the agent and their actions, and, along with the loss of visibility of this link, responsibility is lost too. You talked about this in *Liquid Surveillance*.[5] If killing with a drone is the same as an action in a videogame, the aseptic gap between the decision to strike and the death that follows it reduces the moral weight of action, purifies it in its essence, disempowers and neutralizes it, reduces the action to technical perfection. And I will add as a corollary of more than secondary importance: without a political, civic and moral code that ties actions to their consequences and responsibility to the agent, public opinion is completely left out, it has no radar, no table of Pythagoras, no basic alphabet to see, understand, judge. It will have, if anything, the outcome of the action, the nudity of numbers, the final sum. What is lost in the various reductive processes is a very simple thing: the trace of events and behaviours, their weight, the substance of facts and therefore of reality, what constitutes a benchmark for evaluating the world, as much on the small scale as on the large.

The substance of facts. Herein lies, in my opinion, that 'clarity' that we are looking for – as you say, 'some understanding', the 'knowledge how to go on'. Not merely the event, but rather the mark that it leaves, the

effect it has, and our ability to gauge all of this, weigh it, judge it. I believe that we are facing a change in the understanding of phenomena, something that mixes together the extension of our faculties but along with that a shift in them, almost a deviation. It could not be any different, especially if we consider that the Internet has not just radically changed communication and connection, but has also changed history, since on the web everything happens in the present; it has changed geography, since everything on the Internet is ubiquitous; it has changed the economy, with digital companies that are worth more than offline businesses; it has changed customs by up-ending the knowledge balance between us and our children. An impressive revolution. Through the multiplication of accesses and connections, this revolution has radically transformed our chances to be informed, or at least to be connected – or perhaps, rather, to be exposed – to information.

Here we are: information comes to us, comes into our pockets, into our tablets, we sneak a peek at it 1,000 times a day on every computer screen, because we are exposed to a marvellous new, unprecedented dustcloud of information. Information has become the new 'green ray' that accompanies and envelops us, inside of which we are walking – to the point that Nicholas Negroponte, founder of the MIT Media Lab, can claim that 'connection is a human right. Every human being, as such, should have access to the internet.'[6] And, in fact, at the thought of not being connected, we feel utterly lost, in the dark, without the keys to our home – or, more precisely, without the keys to get out of our home. But we must keep remembering that the world is not in a socket and that behind every connection lies a crossroads, and behind that crossroads lies a land, and that land has a landscape and that landscape a history. It is one thing to skip everything and sum it up into a link, it is quite another to know that land, landscape and history, even at the astonishing speed of our journey. Who will be better informed in the end?

Before we come up with an answer, we must question the meaning of the word. There is a difference between looking and watching, just as there is a difference between knowing and understanding. Being exposed to information – even frequently, everywhere, perhaps unwillingly – does not automatically entail understanding a situation. Understanding the world, in the sense of having it at hand online, easily tameable at the click of a mouse, is a fantastic prerogative, but it does not automatically imply understanding in the sense of deciphering the world, 'getting it'. Even in navigating, there is always the chance to 'buscar el Levante por el Poniente' ('seek the East by way of the West'). The increase of information to levels never witnessed before in the history of mankind is revolutionary in itself, in that it means easy access, plurality of sources, pluralism. But in order to understand the events and know the phenomena, information is not enough: something more is required. I call this 'organized information', a mechanism of knowledge able to grasp a narrative in its unity and in its completeness, from its origin to its climax and its end, recovering the triggering events, projecting them onto their consequences, shedding light on the legitimate and illegitimate interests that give life to the story. And adding the most precious thing: an idea.

This is what a newspaper does: it deconstructs facts, shows the pieces out of which they are made, and builds them up again, adding voices, testimonies, photographs, ideas and, lastly, some comment. Not in order to convert or recruit the reader, since a newspaper is not a priest or a party, but so as to help the reader grasp the dynamics of a fact through this organized path, to understand what motivates it and, most importantly, form a personal opinion. In order to do this, the newspaper should not be an automatic reflection of reality – this is the point – but its interpreter, capable of recreating reality by interpreting the times we are living in, and giving an overall reading of a moment, by the search for a centre of gravity and a global vision. Thus, rather than a source of information, the newspaper is always an autonomous machine of knowledge that collects and selects the facts and gives a new interpretation to what is happening, reading it and making it intelligible, and then organizing it again into a new narrative made of words, images and the context that keeps the whole together and orders it again, harmonizing it into a coherent view.

The fundamental operation here is precisely the creation of context, which zooms out and explains, evokes and paints the 'dark and stormy night' – that is to say, the imaginary scene that can turn Snoopy from a simple dog into a megalomaniac hero. The construction of context is what makes facts intelligible, in that it creates a hierarchy, it relates them to each other, it finds connections and denounces voids, it traces a narrative around a fact, a world around a narrative. It snatches the event from the monopoly of the moment in which it takes place and forces it to last longer and develop, often revealing, in the process, its hidden facets, which overturn the dynamics of expectations. It is like taking a fact, cleaning it of its stereotypes (which, according to Marshall McLuhan, is necessary in order to 'fish' for the fact, isolating it from the current of reality that is constantly changing), shaking it and examining it, only to incline it critically and then grasp the deposit of hidden meaning, at the bottom, where the naked eye cannot see anything, where the spotlights of TV cameras do not reach. And that meaning is what William Carlos Williams calls 'the strange phosphorus of the life'.[7]

This explains why, if the web quenches the thirst for information like no other source, the good old newspaper sates the hunger for knowledge, working as a network of understanding, which led Neil Postman to write that democracy has a 'typographic mind', insofar as the mind of the citizen/voter/newspaper-reader is typographic.[8] The information system is now all one, luckily, but the laws that govern it are to some extent quite different. Thus, information on the web is enormously valuable since it realizes a dream that seemed impossible – telling what is happening right now, in real time – and its form is necessarily that of a flow. With flows, as much as with rivers, what counts is the discharge capacity and the speed of the current, since everything flows in the current; a passage by Habermas and an anonymous quip will travel together into eternity, without anything to distinguish them. The newspaper, on the contrary, keeps one foot in the flow and the other out of it, does not collect everything – it lets most of it flow with the current. But with the pieces of news that it selects every day, it builds a sort of cathedral that gives to its visitors a perception of the events, the richness and complexity of the day that we have just lived, only a part of which we were able to experience in person. In order to perform this discretional and

arbitrary operation of selection and re-creation of reality, the newspaper follows a precise criterion: it extracts
from the flow of the day the news that is most meaningful and best able to cast a significant light on reality.
It is on this sediment of substance that knowledge is
founded, as well as the construction of an opinion, and
also the autonomy of citizens that Bertrand Russell calls
'immunity to eloquence'[9] – that is to say, the capacity to
resist the false magic of the words of Power.

But what reality must we recreate? This substance we
are after, what is it made of? Is it not just a magic trick
(albeit one that is power-less), this belief of ours in the
value of knowledge as the basis of a kind of citizenship
that appears so out of joint? As I write these things in
which I believe, a doubt, as you see, is working its way
into my thoughts. The revolution of spatiality triggered
by globalization, together with the technological revolution, has produced the explosion of modern spatiality
– national, social, political space – disintegrating popular
sovereignty and public sovereignty, making effectively
impossible any control over mandates and any limit
to representation. The phantasmagorical system of the
media pervades the new common space, without organizing it, without ever being able to give it a political
dimension. It is your Pandemonium. As happened in
Babel, tongues chase each other and overlap, items of
news replace each other before they can produce an
idea. 'News', says Todd Gitlin, 'concerns the *event*, not
the underlying condition; the *person*, not the group;
conflict, not consensus; the fact that "*advances the
story*", not the one that explains it'.[10]

This has a very precise meaning, which concerns the
way in which we think, and, more specifically, the way

in which we think politically: the deconstruction of context. But in a world without context, a thousand pieces of information do not add up to knowledge – everything is judged as it happens because only the current exists and, as it unfolds, it justifies itself, since the performance is worth more than its meaning. In this neutralization of the space–time relationship, where the citizen is utterly lost, power takes its revenge on the only counter-power that I know of: the person who wants to know for the sake of knowing, understanding and, lastly, judging.

ZB 'You are not the one who decides that you can do it [. . .] [I]f science can do it, then it is right to do so.' Indeed, you are again on target. Stanley Milgram, a Yale University researcher,[11] asked students at this highly prestigious university – ostensibly well-bred, intelligent and knowledgeable people – to deliver 400-volt-strong, and so severely painful, electric shocks to the objects of an allegedly scientific study of the learning process; 65 per cent followed the command (to the bewilderment and consternation of the learned experts, who expected, at the utmost, 5 per cent to agree!). The shockingly high percentage of ordinary decent people ready to obey the revolting command and administer extreme pain to other human beings has subsequently been explained by the participants' respect for science: the command-giver represented, after all, the highest-calibre expertise, endorsed moreover by one of the most venerable temples of scholarship, and gave commands in the name of scientific research, which meant that the commands must've been serving – mustn't they? – a noble purpose. In another experiment, differently structured but aimed at investigating the same issue, Philip Zimbardo of

Stanford University arrived at equally ghastly results.[12] In both cases, distribution of the responses had the shape of the bell-like 'Gauss curve': a small minority refused explicitly or obliquely, by evasion, to follow commands they found outrageous; at the other extreme, a similarly small minority embraced the sudden licence for cruelty with enthusiastic zeal – but the bulk of the participants simply suspended their own judgements and obeyed docilely the voice of authority. Interestingly, Christopher Browning in his research into another bunch of 'ordinary men' – of a different sort, conscripted to the German 101 Auxiliary Police Battalion and commanded to murder Jews in the Lublin region of Poland (in reality, not in a situation contrived in a psychological laboratory) – found the same pattern of responses[13] – though in that case not the authority of science, but generalized obedience to 'superiors as such', to 'people in command', 'people who know better', caused that effect. What counted ultimately in all those cases was the relief from the burden of responsibility which conformity and compliance offered: the authority of the command-givers to command, as well as their right to require discipline, were assumed and accepted all the more gladly for shifting responsibility onto their shoulders.

I believe that the evasion of responsibility is a common denominator in the above cases of obedience to extreme commands in extreme situations, just as in the swarm-like conduct so widely noted in our notoriously multi-vocal and risk-pregnant 'normality'. Carrying responsibility for one's own choices made among perceived behavioural options, and carrying it under conditions of disorientation and in a cacophony of all-too-often contradictory voices (all haggling for attention and obedience as if on a Kuwaiti bazaar), may prove to be, and often is, an awesome, uncomfortable and, for those reasons, extensively and intensively resented burden. No wonder that so many humans on so many occasions prick up their ears upon hearing offers of relief from that burden – particularly if the pledge on offer is straightforward while the actions it requires in exchange are temptingly, even if deceptively, simple, easy to accomplish and call for little effort and no sacrifice (such as, for instance, rounding up the 'foreigners' and sending them back to 'where they came from'). This is why your recommendation that, 'in order to understand the events and know the phenomena', something more than getting raw information is required – namely consideration of the mark the 'fact' is bound to make on our and other people's lives, as well as developing the 'ability to gauge all of this, weigh it, judge it' – is so timely and crucially important.

You rightly observe that newspapers, thanks to the unique discursive and reflexive qualities of the printed word, stand much more chance of achieving and delivering that 'something more' than do other information media, relying mostly on images. I'd add to your multifaceted analysis of the newspaper's advantage just one more point. Readers of newspaper articles are aware that what they get is not just a glimpse/snapshot of an event – as between the events and their perception someone, a thinking and interpreting author of the report, has already intervened; they are also aware that the author(s) do not stop at telling them that something happened here or there, but aim at imparting comprehension of its causes and possible consequences. Regular readers may well acquire and develop a constant hunger and demand for 'seeing the forest behind the trees': to perceive the world they inhabit, and to whose continuous existence and changing shape they contribute, as an organic totality with its own logic, mechanism and dynamics. Not so the watchers of a video of the event broadcast on a TV screen or downloaded to an iPhone: the ubiquitous presence of, and the designating/ordaining role played by, the camera-people, who do their own interpretative work by aiming their cameras selectively following their own preconceived criteria, is hardly – if at all – noticed in the course of perception; the viewers get a (misleading) impression that what they are facing, seemingly point-blank, is 'the truth of the matter' unmediated, pure and unadulterated, standing on its own and – if you watch attentively – containing everything one needs 'to be informed': indeed, for 'knowing it all', being 'knowledgeable'.

In fact, however, *all* information, from *whatever* media, comes to us 'pre-interpreted': what is presented as the 'facts of the matter' reaches us pre-shaped by the selectively – and therefore, in principle, contentiously – confined (spatial and temporal) contexts. They should demand for that reason reflection, and trigger an argument and debate. Newspapers – and, more generally, the printed word as such – tend to render that status of information visible, enabling/promoting thereby accretion of wisdom arising from the broadening of cognitive horizons. Their electronic replacements, on the other hand, may, and do, tend to cover up that status – suggesting (even if implicitly) the redundancy of reflection and debate, and leading thereby to a shrinking of horizons and impoverishment of understanding. As you rightly comment, 'a thousand pieces of information do not add up to knowledge'; nor do, in our society of exponentially rising multitudes of information and a fast-dwindling and shrivelling volume of comprehension, those millions of websites that Google suggests we consult, when prompted by our inquiry. The newspaper, which, as you say, 'keeps one foot in the flow and the other out of it', and so 'snatches the event from the monopoly of the moment', is better positioned to stop the rot. But will that suffice? The odds against successful defence of proper comprehension are, let's admit, overwhelming. In our society, which boasts of having broken all and any limits to 'data gathering', our understanding of the world we shape while being shaped by it faces up to a truly formidable adversary.

There is one more tremendously important point you so dexterously bring to our attention: in a society whose average member spends more than half of her/his waking time in front of electronic screens, 'at the thought of not being connected, we feel utterly lost, in the dark, without the keys to our home – or, more precisely, without the keys to get out of our home'. *The Blair Witch Project*, a 1999 American horror film written, directed and edited by Daniel Myrick and Eduardo Sánchez, and thought to be the first widely released movie marketed primarily on the Internet,[14] owes its exceptional fame and a fabulous financial success (it is believed to have thus far grossed $248,639,099 worldwide) to its chiming with deeply ingrained – if hidden and subconcious – terrors haunting the generation brought up in our society of 'loners constantly in touch'. The drama narrated by that film of three young film-makers on an expedition to an allegedly haunted wood (though one in close proximity to ordinary American villages and townships) starts with 'losing the connection'; with the realization that their mobile phones are no longer usable due to a lack of signal, and that therefore the protagonists in the narrative cannot find their way back to their vehicle and 'realize they are now hopelessly lost', this drama turns into a hair-rising and blood-curdling horror story. There are mysterious sounds they can't decipher, and baffling signs of a recondite presence they can't pinpoint and ascribe to any – whether friendly or hostile – beings. They have visibly lost the skills of solving the mysteries of life on their own, with no help from messages sent and received. Without gadgets offering instant communication with other gadget-holders, the three youngsters are, purely and simply, hapless and helpless – in fact, as the abrupt ending of the film suggests, doomed. We may say now that their trajectory as (prophetically?) displayed in the film pre-figured and presaged our present lot: the plight of electronics-dependent existence in a time in which communication has supplanted – mutilated, knocked out – understanding.

EM   What you grasp is the point of crisis. Or rather, it is the point where technological revolution meets organized information. Or, in other words: the point where communication and comprehension clash. 'Seeing the forest behind the trees' threatens to become more important than the possibility – here and now – of looking at the trees in person, of moving among them, feeling the leaves rustling in the wind, touching them. Perception includes all other intellectual functions, it becomes the supreme faculty. I perceive, therefore I am. I am in the right place, therefore I understand. So long as I can be there, I do not need anything else. I perceive, therefore I know, and I know only that which

I perceive, because this is the only thing I trust in and feed on: what brings me inside the flow is of some value. What lets me rest on the bank, allowing me to observe the flow, measure it, judge it, is of less value: it is boring, not immediate, not ever-changing, it does not go at the speed to which I am now accustomed. On that bank, there may be experience (which is formed inside the flow and outside of it), there may be skill, in some cases there may be science, and, lastly, there may be the knowledge and even the consciousness of phenomena – fair enough, but all of this does not flow, does not run; quite the contrary, it keeps me there and slows me down, since I too am in the flow, I want to be in it, I too am the flow. And in the flow lies all, or at least all I need.

Flowing and floating means becoming, letting oneself be lulled by the constantly renewing waves, being constantly stimulated by new sensations that keep moving things away from us and leave but a few fixed points. It is clear that in this continuous mutation, perception changes too: a new culture is born, a different way of being in the world, not only of reading and interpreting it. I want to know, of course; and never has knowing been as accessible and easy as today. But what I want to know is that which moves with me and around me in this precise moment, because what counts happens now, and I too perceive myself as a privileged node of the universal connection in constant motion.

There is clearly something grand, titanic even, in this replacement of observation by perception. How could one be oblivious to it? With a click, 'I' am in the middle of events: in just a few seconds, I can watch a video of Taliban attacks on a children's school in Pakistan, and

I can reply to Madonna's tweets about her charities, as if she were talking to me. I am the protagonist, I feel the flow around me, it infects me and is infected by me, I am part of everything: from reader-spectator, I have become navigator on the same stream where the facts happen – I have fully dived into them. I will never get out to dry on the bank again. The technological intermediation to which you refer (behind the images, behind the news, behind the message) is of no interest since it evaporates, such is the force of the focus: here and now, where I am, there lies 'the truth of the matter'. The fact that this so-called 'reality' 'reaches us pre-shaped by the selectively – and therefore, in principle, contentiously – confined (spatial and temporal) contexts' does not count: perception can do away with it or exclude it. If the facts happen now, I can master them. I am there, therefore nothing can deceive me.

But opinion, as such, cannot be reduced to just another part of the flow, it must somehow dominate it, evaluate it, discriminate between its components. We have already said that the newspaper tries to do precisely this. If we consider how it operates inside and outside the flow, discarding and selecting and developing as we have seen, we are able to grasp the shift from the shock of perception to the development of cognition: the gradual construction of a road to understanding events with different elements that are joined to the naked fact – the interview, the analysis, the background, the comment. These are developed pieces of reality, since the newspaper is part of life, not of its representation. Fragments of knowledge that extend the 'here' to a greater context, by expanding the background until it emerges in all clarity, and extend the 'now', by re-constructing it, seeking causes and precedents, wondering as to the consequences of a story. It is a cognitive mechanism that progressively joins to the facts new elements of understanding and interest, identifies new dynamics – it even tries to find the facts' morality, which is the common touchstone of every judgement, great or small. It is what we call 'organized information': an event takes place; a reconstruction is developed and arranged by the newspaper and its related websites; the final idea emerges in me through all of this, through information that becomes knowledge.

It is clear that the moving logic of the flow and its immediate perceptional representation reject precisely this kind of organization. More than that, they reject any mediation whatsoever, regarding it as illegitimate, parasitic, misleading or even openly deceptive. If I am inside the current in which all this takes place, I want to perceive it directly, on my skin and with all my senses; therefore, I want no filters. Even experience becomes a filter. Even skills. Even professionalism. Even development. All that functioned as a safeguard mechanism before the Internet collapses with the Internet. It is inevitable: if the web hurls me into the middle of the action, turning me into the protagonist or at least into a witness, I trust more in my testimony than in that of witnesses by profession. If I am out of the moving phenomena and the web takes me inside them, well, I want to be in them as their master: I acknowledge no external authority. If I can access information on an event as it unfolds, I do not need anything else – no before, no after – and thus not even a certification of good or correct information. I no longer make use of the machinery of information, I am in the machinery. The revolution is Copernican; nobody can take me back to the previous state of customer-reader. I have entered the movie, I will not return among the audience.

Clay Shirky takes it one step further, warning us that around this new movie pivots our entire social structure. Of course, he warns us, 'Our social tools remove older obstacles to public expression, and thus remove the bottlenecks that characterized mass media.'[15] Indeed, we cannot ignore the fact that 'An individual with a camera or a keyboard is now a nonprofit of one, and self-publishing is now the normal case.' But 'The result is the mass amateurization of efforts previously reserved for media professionals', since professions exist 'because there is a scarce resource that requires ongoing management', and a profession 'becomes, for its members, a way of understanding their world'. At the same time, by necessity, the definition of the concept of news itself changes too 'from news as an institutional prerogative to news as part of a communications ecosystem, occupied by a mix of formal organizations, informal collectives, and individuals'. But since mass professionalization is an oxymoron, 'since a professional class implies a specialized function, minimum tests for competence, and a minority of members', the future of the web is this mass amateurization, which entails a shift of perspective (from 'why publish it?' to 'why not publish it?') and therefore a filtering problem, which Shirky regards as incommensurably larger than the one we had with traditional media: 'Filter-then-publish, whatever its advantages, rested on a scarcity of media that is a thing of the past. The expansion of social media means that the only working system is publish-then-filter.' And: 'The media landscape is transformed, because personal communication and publishing, previously separate functions, now shade into one another. One result is to break the older pattern of professional filtering of the good from the mediocre before publication; now such filtering is increasingly social, and happens after the fact.'

I even think that the good and the mediocre, in the marketplace of the web, are endowed with qualities that are, of course, different, but almost of the same value, provided that they can raise the tide and provoke the user. On social networks, a 140-character deconstruction of any argument whatsoever is much more successful than the kind of thinking that may not be as effective in info-capsule form. What works on the web has more value than what is convincing. Herein lies a genuinely revolutionary force, in the sense that it is subversive, almost like a seizure of power. While the privilege that was accorded to professionalism is lost, the pulpit – that privileged post that gives and guarantees recognized authority – is lost as well. It is the end of hierarchy, of the verticality of information, in the name of the horizontality of communication. On social media we are equal, and for this reason we have the impression that we are moving on a freer and more democratic landscape, without monopolies, elites, reserves of power. When Nicolas Sarkozy goes to shake hands physically with his two-millionth Facebook follower, he means precisely this: 'one man, one vote', together we are millions, your opinion counts as much as mine, 'the social' makes equal what is different in the real world.

But let's take a step farther: on social media, we are not only equal in appearance, but we will soon become 'more equal' in actuality. Indeed, in the web's universe, I am doomed to select the most famous names, then the most eye-catching, but most of all – this is the trend that is of greater consequence – I will choose, quickly and continuously, the ones that are more similar to me, that gratify me the most and that seem to give legs and body, extension, mass and quantity to my own thoughts. I will seek numbers – the new informational cabala – and hence, by default, texture and substance. But a substance made of assimilated, selected, comformist thoughts. Thoughts that may easily add up, and be crunched into numbers once again. Until, suddenly, in freedom, in the infinite horizontality of the communicational relation, in the democratic ideal of 'one man, one vote', the first cracks start to appear. Between my mouse that discards opinions that disagree with mine and my pride pleased with the opinions that agree with it, there lies the invisible bottleneck through which I am funnelling down, made of reassuring signals, comforting messages, confirmative thinking. We tend to live and browse among our equals, but the concept of equality from the nineteenth and twentieth centuries has changed its meaning. Today it is not social, not political, not economical. Equality now merely means agreement. An agreeing world around me: everything else is left outside, on distant orbits, losing 'those who move between social sets', as Walter Lippmann put it. They are not the 'augurs', 'custodians', 'interpreters' of a social model, but 'vertically the actual binding together of society', since they establish com-munication channels between different social sets, they provoke and contaminate, they cut and stitch.[16]

It must be true, then, in the end, that 'when we change the way we communicate, we change society', as Shirky writes, changing ourselves in relation to others.[17] We choose – or think we choose – the contexts in which we prefer to amble, and meanwhile we break the single con-text that until recently used to make up our reference points, our common landscape, our shared background. And thus, in this organized disintegration, 'comprehend-ing what we have in common with others', as Tony Judt writes, is 'an increasing difficulty', all focused as we are on 'form[ing] global communities of elective affinity – while losing touch with the affinities of our neighbors'.[18] At this point we may conclude, with Castells: 'In our society, the protocols of communication are not based on the sharing of culture but on the culture of sharing.'[19] And here the first doubts arise. If it is true that 'power is relational, domination is institutional', we are no longer able to challenge that dominion with our opin-ions, which are chopped up, fragmented and reduced to numbers; as to relations, if they are so severely divided, selected and distinct, what kind of power could they ever produce, what security of belonging, of value, of opinion? The director Werner Herzog cuts to the chase:

> The internet has no structure. But the structure must lie in you. To understand things you must understand their grammar. Only in this way will you be able to move through this amorphous mass of information. In order to do so, you must have a cultural, ideological and informa-tional structure, and this is what young people lack the most, since they do not read enough. This loss of cultural grammar is one of the reasons why people today live with a constant sense of loss. In the internet they lose themselves and they lose things.[20]

I am not as pessimistic as Herzog and I am not as convinced that the key lies outside reality and outside the web, exclusively within ourselves.

Looking for the core of things, a sediment of significance that may be valid for everyone for ever, even in the digital AD, I have taken shelter, as you have seen, in the search for meaning. But, after all we have said, here too an abyss opens up and the contagion – Herzog's 'loss' – spreads. Provided we seriously want to seek it, where does meaning lie nowadays? What is the meaning of things made of? The meaning, does it still have the same meaning? Maybe our Zeitgeist is something else, its opposite: not having a defined and recognizable meaning, not looking for it, not demanding it. Be happy with the signs.

ZB 'Flowing and floating means becoming', you observe. Indeed, in the wake of the all-too-visible and all too often painfully experienced weakening and untying of sound and sturdy, non-negotiable bonds having transformed 'identity' from a 'given' into a task, the work of 'becoming' turns simultaneously possible and all-but unavoidable. Fighting back – not to mention resisting effectively – the progressive disassembly of closely knit communities and a new frailty of belonging has proved for many reasons an uphill struggle.

As in the case of so many other of life's mischiefs and calamities, the Internet comes, handily, to help – especially in one feat in which it excels more than in any other: the stunt of cleansing action of the discomforts and inconveniences it might entail if undertaken offline – in that area widely, though debatably, called 'real life'. Constructing an offline *community* is a forbiddingly difficult and at times dangerous assignment, but patching together an online *network* (or for that matter overhauling it or taking it apart if found short of bringing full satisfaction) is childishly (I mean it literally) facile. There is, in addition, no limit to the number and diversity of networks that an internaut can compose and concurrently hold (and 'belong' to); one can therefore take up and discard any sort of unfamiliar and untested, tentative and probationary identities with little, if any, risk – most importantly, avoiding the ballast of long-term, not to mention interminable, commitments. It is obvious that this advantage of online networks and online identities portends ill for the hopes and trials of arresting the erosion and disintegration of their offline counterparts – on whose performance they were meant to improve and whom they were augured eventually to replace. And so – continually enticed and seduced by the ever-renewing richness of the current, of the real time, as you imply, and forced or beguiled (in most cases both) by the necessity and chance of 'becoming', to join in that 'flowing and floating' – 'I too am the flow.' Capitulating to overwhelming pressures, or internalizing those pressures and recycling them in one's own will and desire, we try to fill with Facebook, that Market of Identities Unlimited, the vacuum left by dissipating social bonds.

That capitulation is not, to be sure, perceived as an unmitigated disaster. Alongside its direct and collateral harms and damages, it has its benefits. One of them, correctly mentioned by you, is the 'mass amateurization, which entails a shift of perspective (from "why publish it?" to "why not publish it?")', and 'self-publishing is now the normal case'. Does it mean, however, that what we are witnessing or can expect 'is the end of hierarchy, of the verticality of information, in the name of the horizontality of communication'? Well, theoretically speaking it could be the case, if not for the fact that in our world, smarting under the omnipotent rule of free markets in their constant search for virgin (read: as yet unexploited and so not profit-bringing) lands to conquer, colonize and transform into profit-factories, circulation of information can hardly expect immunity from commercialization. Commercialization in its extreme form, that of monopoly stifling competition – and especially 'amateurish' competition, daring to confront point-blank the dominant market forces and engage them in battle – is in full swing. Three publishing giants – Elsevier, Springer and Wiley-Blackwell – divided between themselves a large, indeed decisive part of scholarly, authoritative publications: namely, the academic journals deemed (because of being peer-reviewed) to carry a collective endorsement by the profession: the must-read, therefore, for everybody engaged in scientific research and teaching, as well as everybody wishing to know and comprehend the current progress and the 'last word' in science. Those giants established in practice a genuine monopoly on speaking with the authority of science – and, by proxy, with the authority of truth, reducing the rest of information attainable on the Internet to the low rank of 'mere opinions' – dubious and unreliable. They erected a monetary wall around their estate, to draw, mark and fortify – indeed, render practically impassable – the border between the dignified, solemn and serene 'authority of truth' and the free-for-all bazaar of haggling peddlers of half-truths and lies. For the privilege of reading one paper from one issue of one of the hundreds of Elsevier's scholarly journals, you'll have to pay $31.50; for a similar privilege, Springer charges €34.95, and Wiley-Blackwell $42. The exorbitant prices charged for annual subscription to the said journals (the average price of which – for instance, for the chemistry journals – is $3,792, whereas the top prices go as high as $20,930) force university librarians to cut expenditure on journal subscription – casting thereby the authoritative sources of tested and endorsed knowledge out of reach of many, perhaps most, university and college libraries and their users; which yet further exacerbates the role of the Internet in rendering access to knowledge more constrained and elitist instead of making it more widely attainable and more democratic. There are strong reasons to suspect that, when it comes to the knowledge-based human capabilities, the Internet is on the whole engaged more in digging moats than building bridges.

Monetary walls are more indomitable and forbidding than those built of concrete or steel. It is downright inconceivable that, in their presence, the democratic, indeed egalitarian potential of 'universal access to the web' could be realized. The market of information cannot be scrutinized and evaluated, let alone managed, separately from two other interconnected markets: of labour or of finances. It can't but be subjected to the superior logic of the latter.

Let me briefly pause on another crucial issue – indeed one of the most hurtful, though ever less noticed, banes of our times: the issue of meaning, graspable solely when related to the grammar hiding behind the thicket of words. You ask: 'Provided we seriously want to seek it, where does meaning lie nowadays? What is the meaning of things made of? The meaning, does it still have the same meaning? Maybe our Zeitgeist is something else, its opposite: not having a defined and recognizable meaning, not looking for it, not demanding it. Be happy with the signs.'

This is not a new question, to be sure; nor a new premonition, nor a new apprehension, which such foreboding can't but cause in many enlightened and critical – critical *because* enlightened – minds. It is thus that our conditions prompt us to dispose of the search for meaning – teaching, training and drilling us to adjust our mode of being-in-the-world to essentially and incurably meaningless surroundings. Or perhaps surroundings that overflow with meanings, for the reason of their sheer numbers, are no longer amenable to being grasped? With myriads of signals leaving us with no time to find out what they are signalling? The merit of being the first to posit this question, which still seeks in vain a conclusive answer, can be ascribed to Georg Simmel, one of the principal founders of modern social science.[21] He in turn ascribed the birth of that question to the existential conditions of a big city – a 'metropolis': more particularly, to the uniquely metropolitan 'blasé attitude'. 'There is perhaps', he wrote, 'no psychic phenomenon which has been so unconditionally reserved to the metropolis as has the blasé attitude':

> The blasé attitude results first from rapidly changing and closely compressed contrasting stimulations of the nerves. [...] A life in boundless pursuit of pleasure makes one blasé because it agitates the nerves to their strongest reactivity for such a long time that they finally cease to react at all. [...] The essence of the blasé attitude consists in the blunting of discrimination.

That blunting is assisted and magnified by 'another source that flows from the money economy'.

And he explains:

> This does not mean that the objects are not perceived, as
> in the case of a half-wit, but rather that the meaning and
> differing values of things, and thereby the things them-
> selves, are experienced as insubstantial. They appear to
> the blasé person in an evenly flat and gray tone: no one
> object deserves preference over any other. This mood is
> the faithful subjective reflection of the completely internal-
> ized money economy. By being the equivalent to all the
> manifold things in one and the same way, money becomes
> the most frightful leveller. [. . .] All things float with equal
> specific gravity in the constantly moving stream of money.

Things, one may conclude, cease having unique meanings of their own and in their own right; they derive
their *raison d'être*, so to speak, from their mutual relations. What matters to the blasé person is their exchange
value – full stop. If meaning is sought at all, it is found –
or at any rate deemed to be found – *outside* the object in
question: in that object's potential for being exchanged
and/or replaced.

Given the tremendous multitude of sounds and sights
that fill and overflow it, the Internet – contrary to
widespread, yet misleading, opinion – does not create
McLuhan's 'global village', but a mega-city: Simmel's
'metropolis'. With iPhones in everybody's pocket and tablets at the stretch of everybody's hand, we find ourselves
– regardless of where our homes are located and whether
we are at the moment at home or out – in a mega-city,
with all the psycho-social consequences prophetically
presaged by Simmel 100 years ago. In mega-cities –
which, apart from being perpetually inundated with an

un-assimilable profusion of nerve stimuli, happen to be as well 'the main seats of money exchange' and, for this reason, 'bring the purchasability of things to the fore much more impressively than do smaller localities' – there is little, if any, room or time for investigating in depth, or for that matter constructing, the specific own meanings of the objects behind the swarm of fleeting and volatile impressions. Those objects, as Simmel points out, nondistinguishable by their specific gravity, dissolve 'in the constantly moving stream' of nerve stimuli and money. We are among those objects. We are those objects. Like the rest of those objects, we seldom pause to reflect; most of us are too busy braving the tides to cogitate about meanings – unless this is a kind of meaning poignantly described in one of Franz Kafka's parables:

> I stand on the end platform of the tram and am completely unsure of my footing in this world, in this town, in my family. Not even casually could I indicate any claims that I might rightly advance in any direction. I have not even any defence to offer for standing on this platform, holding on to this strap, letting myself be carried by this tram, nor for the people who give way to the tram or walk quietly along or stand gazing into shopwindows. Nobody asks me to put up a defense, indeed, but that is irrelevant.[22]

This is hammered home in another:

> No one, no one at all, can blaze a trail to India. Even in his day the gates to India were beyond reach, yet the King's sword pointed the way to them. Today the gates have receded to remoter and loftier places, no one points the way; many carry swords, but only to brandish them, and the eye that tries to follow them is confused.[23]

Evidently, Kafka falls in with your suspicion that presently the meaning of meaning is 'not having a defined and recognizable meaning, not looking for it, not demanding it. Be happy with the signs.'

EM The signs replace the sense, then. Now that the world is entirely known and completely reproducible, it almost seems possible for us to content ourselves with perusing it through its traces, marks and symbols – signs, of course – trying to find in the representation what we used to seek in the production of meaning: as though, instead of travelling across the world, we were happy with spinning a globe. We are left with the name of the thing, and the sign that springs from it. All the rest (essence, substance, relation) does not count, like that 'grammar hiding' – as you remind us – 'behind the thicket of words'. We have reached the Mephistopheles stage: the word completely replaces the thought.

But, actually, the word too is reduced more and more to a sign, or at least a signal: think only of the inflated use of acronyms. Yesterday, the medium was the message; today, the medium can do without the message. Young people now exchange empty messages with their phones just to say hi, poke, confirm; impulses are the ultimate synthesis of word and nothingness, and confound them. Besides, if your identity is that of a point in a network and your system is made of nodes, then the vital issue is to pulsate, to participate in the great heartbeat rather than in the old debate, not to miss the beat, not to leave the circle. Feeling is more necessary than understanding; it becomes more natural, it is one's prerogative, not an effort. At the centre of the web – everyone is at the centre and at the periphery of the web

– I live in connection with people's emotions, friends' sensations, strangers' reactions, with the information of the flow, the selections produced by social networks, the 'swarm of fleeting and volatile impressions', as you say. I feel, therefore I am. I am online, therefore I feel.

More precisely, what should I do while I live in full immersion and I am carried by what you call 'tides'? I believe that the idea is precisely this: I perceive. It is a process that lies midway between the physical and the intellectual, in the sense that I intercept, receive, feel and participate. I look at the images, I welcome confessions, I eschew insults, I receive emotions, I download songs, I put myself in the hands of the information that Facebook or Twitter favoured and guaranteed, feeding it with 'followers' and 'likes' by a giant yet exclusive word-of-mouth. Cognition, in the traditional sense of the term, is replaced by perception. I absorb, therefore I know. No matter that I am receiving what I know through a bundle of emotion-information-sensation rather than by reflecting on the phenomena. And thus the symbol attracts me more than its meaning, because it refers me to the invisible, the imagination, the incompleteness, and it short-circuits meaning into meta-meaning: because the symbol, as Lippmann said, 'secure[s] unity and flexibility without real consent [. . .]. It obscures personal intention, neutralizes discrimination [. . .], it welds [the] group [. . .] to purposeful action. It renders the mass mobile though it immobilizes personality.'[24]

This constantly renewing sensory, expressive and perceptive process is founded on impressions rather than notions, but I would not go as far as saying that it is a wholesale reduction of the epistemological mechanism. To some extent, on the contrary, it upgrades it, in new ways taken in new directions, as we shall see. It certainly takes the epistemological mechanism apart and builds it up differently, making it operate along lines that are completely different from the ones to which we were accustomed. Online, we all become receptors and conductors of the information – big or small – that reaches us and transits through us only to carry on to who knows where. We receive, indeed, we absorb, to the point where we reach the paradox of Nicholas Negroponte's latest prophecy, according to which, one day, 'we will ingest knowledge, swallow it like a pill, it will reach our brain through the blood stream',[25] thus skipping all the personal, individual, autonomous and critical processes of learning, including the relationship between teacher and learner. But, as Dante said, 'non fa scienza, / sanza lo ritenere, avere inteso' ('understanding without retaining makes up no knowledge'). Absorbing is different from learning, finding nourishment is not just consuming, growing is a path that we cannot run through in a second. Along the way, my relationship with knowledge changes, what I learn affects who I am, but I too use what I learn for my concrete actions; I bring what I learn to my everyday life, I exploit it, use it as a tool in the literal and material sense of the term, to the point of Brecht's aphorism: 'Go search for knowledge, you who are freezing.' In other words, life is a lot more than a pill. And man shall not live by chemistry alone.

There is a kind of extremist consistency in these ideas that is brand new and nearly fanatical, as though, with the web, reality had already been completely revealed, knowledge were all at hand, and wisdom were something to download rather than to achieve and discover – like a new Book or Kabbalah, which contains the secret formula to everything and only needs opening. Life is conceived as a giant Wikipedia, capable of tremendous expansion, a horizontal Tower of Babel that tends to infinity, or rather totality, and that gives its definition to everything that deserves to be 'in', excluding everything that is 'out' only because it does not fit into Instagram's open and universal collection – such as the matter of things, the human factor, the alliance between a fact, a concept, the idea that springs from it and, indeed, their meaning. Finally, the world is as flat as it was once said to be, and everything has already been told. One need only connect to prevent what is unforeseeable, find comfort in what has already been said and thought, have all the answers even when we have no questions any more: what use are they? Then Ebola suddenly breaks out, to confuse at once past nightmares with present fears, and we find out that the unforeseeable cannot be prevented, that the world cannot be reduced to a single dimension. As it once was with the Towers, taken down as easily as in a videogame by those who had decided to fly just under the shadow-line of Western thought, of the cost–benefit reckoning of every action, of Cartesian rationalism, or, in other words, of our usual relation between order and chaos. Even as early as 1970, there were those who, like Michel Foucault, encouraged us, saying that:

> we must not resolve discourse into a play of pre-existing significations; we must not imagine that the world turns towards us a legible face which we would have only to decipher; the world is not the accomplice of our knowledge; there is no prediscursive providence which disposes the world in our favour. We must conceive discourse as a violence which we do to things [. . .].[26]

But it is undeniable that, in this oracular universe (I know I can find everything, even though I do not know what I am looking for, or why), a particular kind of culture is developing, which shapes and equips that 'new kind of human being' you refer to, quoting Serres. I do not know whether you happen to have read the recent interview with the Nobel laureate Andre Geim. It is impressive. He imagines that:

> we will not survive in our current form. We will evolve into a new one. We are already evolving. The new form is known as 'global society'. It is a creature infinitely more complex than the old *Homo sapiens*. Human beings are contained within it like the molecules that make up matter. *Homo sapiens* has lasted roughly fifty-thousand years. We will see what this new creature, global society, will become in another fifty-thousand years.'[27]

If we put together what we said about the culture of signs and signals, the pulsating, feeling, perceiving, understanding through emotion, we may catch a glimpse of the embryo of the change that is under way: this is the predisposition of a kind of new 'sixth sense', if it is indeed true, as Walter Benjamin said, that 'During long periods of history, the mode of human sense perception changes with humanity's entire mode of existence' because 'The manner in which human sense perception is organized, the medium in which it is accomplished, is determined not only by nature but by historical circumstances as well.'[28] This 'sixth sense' simplifies. It catalogues. It selects. It includes and excludes. It constantly watches what it is shown and reacts to this, convinced that it is everything – or, at any rate, that it is enough. It intercepts. It consents and

Babel

dissents. It multiplies. It spreads. It cancels. It records sensations. It technicizes impressions. It puts emotions in a bottle, as we used to do with miniature ships. In other words, this 'sixth sense' allows one to be always on the crest of the wave of our choosing; it gives one the prerogative to visit different worlds, coming and going as one pleases; it gives us the impression that we are constantly exercising our judgement on everything, and therefore mastering the whole, sitting at the head of the table. Except that we then look up and realize that everyone is sitting at the head of the table, and therefore this table is as infinite and round as in an illusion.

And so let us ask: are we really still capable of judging? This feeling of power and freedom is the essential ingredient of the Internet culture. But in Simmel's metropolis, as you quote, 'the essence [. . .] consists in the blunting of discrimination'. Perpetually inundated 'with an un-assimilable profusion of nerve stimuli', there is little if any room or time 'for investigating in depth, or [. . .] constructing, the specific own meanings of the objects' that 'dissolve "in the constantly moving stream"'. You come to the conclusion that 'we seldom pause to reflect; most of us are too busy braving the tides to cogitate about meanings'. Indeed, we produce stimuli – only rarely concepts: suggestions, rather than cogitations. This is regardless of Castells' claims that 'There is no opposition between cognition and emotion' because 'Political cognition is emotionally shaped' and 'citizens make decisions by managing conflicts (often unconscious) between their emotional condition (how they feel) and their cognitive condition (what they know)'. When the conflict sharpens, 'people tend to believe what they want to believe'. And 'even in an economic crisis, it is an individual's emotional response to the crisis, rather than a reasoned calculation of how best to respond to the crisis, that organizes people's thinking and political practice'.[29]

Living in connection with the emotions of the world, inside the great collective feeling, can thus expand our perceptive instrumentation. But what are we to do with it? Sensations, perceptions, impressions, emotions do not constitute a public opinion. The structure of web citizenship reminds one, rather, about that of the 'crowd' sketched by Gustave Le Bon as early as 1895:

> Under certain given circumstances, and only under those circumstances, an agglomeration of men presents new characteristics very different from those of the individuals composing it. The sentiments and ideas of all the persons in the gathering take one and the same direction, and their conscious personality vanishes. A collective mind is formed, doubtless transitory, but presenting very clearly defined characteristics.

Indeed, 'Any display of premeditation by crowds is [. . .] out of the question. They may be animated in succession by the most contrary sentiments, but they will always be under the influence of the exciting causes of the moment. They are like the leaves which a tempest whirls up and scatters in every direction and then allows to fall.' But let us keep following Le Bon while thinking of our times:

> though the wishes of crowds are frenzied, they are not durable [. . .]. A crowd is not merely impulsive and mobile. [. . .] [I]t is not prepared to admit that anything can come between its desire and the realisation of its desire,

in consequence of the feeling of irresistible power given it by its numerical strength. The notion of impossibility disappears for the individual in a crowd. [. . .] Whatever be the ideas suggested to crowds they can only exercise effective influence on condition that they assume a very [. . .] simple shape.

This may be translated into images that 'may take each other's place like the slides of a magic lantern'. Crowds 'are devoid of the notion of improbability' which:

in a general way [is] the most striking. This is why it happens that it is always the marvellous and legendary side of events that more specially strike crowds [. . .]. Appearances have always played a much more important part than reality in history, where the unreal is always of greater moment than the real [. . .]. It is not, then, the facts in themselves that strike the popular imagination, but the way in which they take place and [. . .] by their condensation [. . .] produce a startling image which fills and besets the mind.[30]

We are talking about more than a century ago, but if the analogy still holds, this is due precisely to the nature of the virtual bond that is formed on the web, where a contact is considered a 'friend', a click becomes a 'like', and what you call 'frailty of belonging' arises from a selection of contacts that is random, skin-deep, fast and, of necessity, hasty. The virtual communities do not possess those 'sound and sturdy, non-negotiable bonds' that in the real world require effort, as you show; groups are not born on the basis of a profound sense of belonging – collective consumerism replaces shared values, the web exchanges signs instead of meanings. That is the reason why the group reminds one of the crowd. And it acts like the crowd too: similarly to the crowd, it re-acts, because action proper takes place only in real life. This is, after all, Evgeny Morozov's thesis: 'Tweets [. . .] do not topple governments; people do' – because, although their power is unlimited, technologies are nothing but 'tools without handles'.[31] 'Twitter, dates and saffron' we once entitled an article by Tahar Ben Jelloun in *La Repubblica* at the time of the Arab Spring, thinking that Google would pave the way to democracy, freedom and rights, and that the social networks would open a thousand cracks in the walls of authoritarianism: democratic cracks, naturally. However, as Morozov says, we must soon realize that the Internet 'penetrates and reshapes all walks of political life, not just the ones conducive to democratisation', but also those advantageous to the powers that be, which may sharpen their systems of propaganda, make surveillance more powerful, manipulate the new media, control public space by turning it to entertainment rather than to politics: 'What if the liberating potential of the Internet also contains the seeds of depoliticization and thus dedemocratization?'

But, yet again: we are the ones to choose – luckily. The Internet changes our lives, but does not determine them. The tool is for our use, we are not for its use. We are the handles. The reserve of a conscious public opinion lies in our desire to understand, our effort to judge, our capability for outrage – when it is necessary, in our faculty to employ what you call 'that extraordinary particle – No'. In order to do this we must exploit the knowledge currently present on the web in all its vastness, immediacy and speed, as well as the web's capacity for redistributing such knowledge to the four corners of the earth, thus creating new mechanisms of perception and relation. But we must keep searching for the meaning of things by walking down the street, talking to real people, measuring the reality of their problems and engagements on their faces. We must not stop asking questions. Of course, it is still difficult nowadays, – because of all the reasons we have discussed from page 1 – to understand what we have in common, and therefore it is difficult to make this opinion 'public', though we hold it precious, because it is ours, because it is our way of reading the world, because it gives meaning to our path among other people as citizens – and not subjects or exiles – of democracy. But it depends on us, on our ability to think, our ability to talk. When Jimmy Page, guitarist in Led Zeppelin, by then in his seventies, was asked the band's secret, this was his answer: 'We didn't try to allay the audience's anxieties. We offered them a concept.' The kingdom of rock for a concept: who would have guessed? To some extent, the indigenous people of Bioko in Equatorial Guinea had suggested as much, using other words, to Ivor Richards and Cecyl Ogden, the two linguists who encountered them on their island: 'Let us get nearer to the fire, so that we can see what we are saying.'[32]

ZB Bronisław Malinowski, one of the principal founders of modern anthropology, coined the concept of phatic expressions – a family name for exclamations of the 'ciao', 'come sta', 'come va', 'salve' or 'benvenuto' kind.[33] The sole information which phatic expressions contain and convey is 'I'm here! And I note you also are here.' They are pleas for attention, un-committal phrases announcing a *chance* of communication, a possibility of an exchange – but neither demands nor firm, binding promises to engage in such: bids without pledges. A genuine contact, intercourse, commerce – a real *encounter* between humans in their capacity of *subjects* – may, though doesn't necessarily have to, follow. Phatic expressions are invitations, with a codicil of RSVP – suggested and expected, though not assured, to follow. Phatic expressions may lead (to borrow Martin Buber's distinction) as much to *Begegnungen* (true encounters) as to *Vergegnungen* (failed or mock encounters).

Jean-Luc Godard, the great French pioneer of the 'new wave' in modern cinema, dedicated his work to debunking the hypocrisy of our daily language, attempting to uncover the true meanings of words dissimulated by dissimulations, false pretences and self-deceptions – words that, having cut themselves free from their originally intended meanings, weave a dense network of images, pre-judgements and stereotypes, obstructing instead of revealing the sense of our motives, deeds and experiences. He did in images what Milan Kundera calls for writers to accomplish in their novels by tearing-up the curtains woven of words. We may view Michael Haneke – most notably in his 2009 masterpiece *Le ruban blanc* – as the present-day heir of Goddard's mission to unravel the drama of divorce between words and meanings – and consequently between meanings and the human way of being-in-the-world. But Goddard himself, at eighty-four, in *Adieu au langage*, summed up his own mission and its final defeat – by presenting a series of unconnected, aimlessly moving images running simultaneously ('in real time') with similarly unconnected words and sentences. For the first 20 or 30 minutes of the film, the viewer waits (in vain, in vain) for a meaningful story to emerge from the chaos of sights and sounds – until the sombre truth dawns upon her or him that there is no story in the succession of images that can be patched together from the succession of words. After divorce, words and meaning settled in two separate, incommunicado universes. And that applies in equal measure to the collection of apparently grave statements gleaned from the common language of politics. The film could be equally well named *Adieu aux significations*.

You observe: 'Young people now exchange empty messages with their phones just to say hi, poke, confirm' – a correct observation. The Internet, through which a great majority of contacts nowadays occurs, is a realm and a nursery of phatic expressions; it discourages and impedes, if not downright prohibits, anything loaded with a graver meaning (as does its most heavily attended branch, Twitter, allowing no more than 140 characters in a message). You conclude: 'Yesterday, the medium was the message; today, the medium can do without the message': a truly razor-sharp sentence, deserving to be as widely distributed and absorbed as that by Marshall McLuhan, which preceded it and is now largely outdated. Indeed, one is tempted to conclude that today's most popular medium not just 'can do without' the message, but cuts the message out, preferably altogether, along with other unnecessarily time-and-brains-taxing inessentials. Whether intentionally or in its effects, online communication all too often acts as an object-lesson in *inessentiality* of meaning.

The next crucial issue is raised by you when you refer to Tahar Ben Jelloun, writing at the time of the Arab Spring, thinking that Google 'would pave the way to democracy'. Ben Jelloun was not alone – by no means! The official American establishment's reaction to the Iranian youth venting briefly, on the streets of Tehran, their protest against the fraudulent elections of June 2009 bore striking resemblance to a commercial campaign on behalf of the likes of Facebook, Google or Twitter. I suppose that some gallant investigative journalist – to whose company, alas, I do not belong – could have supplied weighty material proofs of this impression. The *Wall Street Journal* pontificated: 'this would not happen without Twitter!' Andrew Sullivan, an influential and well-informed American blogger, pointed to Twitter as 'the critical tool for organizing the resistance in Iran', whereas the venerable *New York Times* waxed lyrical, proclaiming a combat between 'thugs firing bullets' and 'protesters firing tweets'.[34] Hillary Clinton went on record announcing, in her 21 January 2010 'Internet Freedom' speech,[35] the birth of the 'samizdat of our day', and proclaiming the need 'to put these tools [meaning 'viral videos and blog posts'] in the hands of people around the world who will use them to advance democracy and human rights'. 'Information freedom', she opined, 'supports the peace and security that provide a foundation for global progress'. (Let me note right away, though, that little water had flowed under the Potomac bridges before the American political elite started – as if following the French injunction of *deux poids, deux mesures* – to demand restrictions on WikiLeaks and a prison sentence for its founder.) Ed Pilkington[36] recalls Mark Pfeiffe, a George Bush adviser who nominated Twitter for a Nobel Prize, and quotes Jared Cohen, an official in the US State Department, who described Facebook as 'one of the most organic tools for democracy the world has ever seen'. To put it in the nutshell: Jack Dorsey, Mark Zuckerberg and their companions-in-arms are the generals of the advancing Democracy-and-Human-Rights Army – and we all, tweeting and sending Facebook messages, are its soldiers. Media is indeed the message – and the message of the digital media is the 'information curtain is descending' and uncovering thereby the new planet-scape of people power and universal human rights.

It is this un-common-sense of the American political and opinion-making elite and other unpaid salespersons of digital services that Evgeny Morozov, then a 26-year-young student and newcomer from Belorussia to America, berated, ridiculed and condemned as a 'net delusion' in his book with the same title.[37] Among many other points Morozov managed to squeeze into his 400-page-long study was that, according to Al-Jazeera, there were but sixty active Twitter accounts in Tehran, and so the organizers of the demos used mostly such shamefully old-fashioned techniques of getting attention as making telephone calls or knocking on their neighbours' doors – but that the clever rulers of autocratic Iran, no less Internet-savvy than ruthless and unscrupulous, looked up on Facebook to find any links to known dissidents, using that information to isolate, incarcerate and disempower the potential leaders of revolt, and nip the democratic challenge to autocracy (if there ever was one) in the bud. And there are many and different ways in which authoritarian regimes can use the Internet to their own advantage, Morozov points out – and many of them did use them and go on using them.

To start with, social networks offer a cheaper, quicker, more thorough and altogether easier way to identify and locate current or potential dissidents than any of the traditional instruments of surveillance. And, as David Lyon argues and attempts to show in our joint study,[38] surveillance-through-social-networks is made so much more effective thanks to the cooperation of its intended objects and victims. We live in a confessional society, promoting public self-exposure to the rank of the prime and most easily available – as well as arguably most potent and the sole truly proficient – proof of social existence. Millions of Facebook users vie with each other to disclose and put on public record the most intimate and otherwise inaccessible aspects of their identity, social connections, thoughts, feelings and activities. Social websites are fields of a voluntary, do-it-yourself form of surveillance, beating hands down (both volume-wise and expenditure-wise) the specialist agencies manned by professionals in spying and detection . . . A true windfall, genuinely pennies-from-heaven-style, for every dictator and his secret services – and a superb complement to the numerous 'banoptical' institutions of democratic society concerned with preventing the unwanted and undeserving (that is, all those who behave or are likely to behave *comme il ne faut pas*) from being mistakenly admitted or worming themselves surreptitiously into our decent self-selected democratic company. One of *The Net Delusion*'s chapters is titled 'Why the KGB wants you to join Facebook'.

Morozov spies out the many ways in which authoritarian – nay, tyrannical – regimes can beat the alleged freedom fighters at their own game, using the technology in which the apostles and panegyrists of the Internet's democratic bias vested their hopes. No news here – old technologies, as the article in *The*

Economist already quoted reminded us, were similarly used by past dictators to pacify and disarm their victims: research showed that East Germans with access to Western television were less likely to express dissatisfactions with the regime. As for the, admittedly much more potent, digital informatics, 'the internet has provided so many cheap and easily available entertainment fixes to those living under authoritarianism that it has become considerably harder to get people to care about politics at all'. That is, unless politics is recycled into another exciting, full of sound and fury yet comfortingly toothless, safe and innocuous, variety of entertainment – something practised by the new generation of 'slacktivists', who believe that 'clicking on a Facebook petition counts as a political act' and so 'dissipate their energies on a thousand distractions', each meant for instant consumption and one-off use, which the Internet is a supreme master of producing and disposing of daily (just one of numberless examples of how effective political slacktivism is at changing the ways and means of the 'real world' is the sad case of the 'Save the Children of Africa' group: it needed several years to collect the princely sum of $12,000, while the un-saved children of Africa went on dying).

With popular mistrust of the powers-that-be spreading and deepening, and popular esteem of the power-to-the-people potential of the Internet rising sky-high through the joint efforts of Silicon Valley marketing and Hillary Clinton-style lyrics recited and broadcast from thousands of academic offices, no wonder that pro-government propaganda has a better chance of being listened to and absorbed if it reaches its targets through the Internet. The more clever among the authoritarians know all too well that this is the case; after all, informatics experts are all too available for hiring, eager to sell their services to the highest bidder. Hugo Chavez is on Twitter, and boasts half a million Facebook friends, while in China there is ostensibly a genuine army of government-subsidiarized bloggers (commonly baptized 'the 50 cents party' for being paid 50 cents for every entry). Morozov keeps reminding his readers that – as Pat Kane puts it – 'patriotic service can be as much a motivation for the young socio-technical operative as the bohemian anarchism of Assange and his pals'. Info-hackers may equally enthusiastically, and with the same volume of good will and sincerity, join a new 'Transparency International' as a new 'Red Brigade'. The Internet would support both choices with equal equanimity.

It is an old, very old story told all over again: one can use axes to hew wood or to cut heads. The choice does not belong to the axes but to those who hold them. Whatever the holders' choices, the axes won't mind. And however sharp the edges which it may currently be cutting, technology would not advance democracy and human rights for (and instead of) you. It is more likely to release you from your citizen's responsibility for advancing them. I believe that it is, paradoxically, the explicit or implicit promise of release from that (no doubt demanding and cumbersome) responsibility that is the main attraction of conducting the political game online. And there is one more difficult-to-resist online temptation: that of replacing the hard necessity for argument with the joyful freedom of hate-speech.

As we know from Sigmund Freud's studies and their follow-up by Norbert Elias, an integral part of modern history was also the 'civilizing process' – consisting in suppressing manifestations of hostility, aggression, cruelty, blood-thirst, or at least eliminating them from view in daily interactions. One of the effects of that process was to render the show of emotions in public shameful – something to be avoided at all costs, in however stressful a situation. Note that the objects of prohibition were the *manifestations* of emotions, not *emotions as such*. Ervin Goffman's 'civic inattention' demanded a demonstrative lack of personal interest in people around (such as avoiding eye contact or close and intrusive physical proximity), rather than a moral reform; that inattention was a stratagem meant to enable cohabitation of strangers in modern, densely populated cities: cohabitation free from mutual violence and fear thereof. It bore all the marks of a cover-up, rather than elimination of mutual enmity and aggressiveness. The civilizing process softened human conduct in public places, rather than making humans more moral, friendly and caring about others.

The modern demand for self-restraint and desisting from violence to others is not, therefore, absolute but conditional, confined to certain kinds of behaviour, certain categories of 'others', and certain sorts of milieux and situations. We are trained daily by the opinion-making media as well as political authorities to treat acts of exclusion, banishment, exile as phenomena so ordinary, frequent and ubiquitous that for all practical intents and purposes they are no longer visible, let alone shocking and disturbing for the moral conscience. The media offer massively popular shows of the *Big Brother* or *Weakest Link* type, in which the repetitive, routine and scheduled séances of exclusion invariably provide the widely cherished and ratings-hoisting highlights – the main foci of interest and, indeed, entertainment. Political authorities, with rising support among their electors, set aside categories of people to whose treatment the canonical commandments do not apply – or apply in a severely cut-down measure: terrorists, people suspected of giving them shelter and so fit for the role of 'collateral casualties' of drones and artillery fire, heretics or members of the wrong kind of sects, illegal immigrants, or the 'underclass' with all their different circumstances – no longer a social problem but a problem of 'asocial behaviour', and therefore of 'law and order'.

The potentially morbid 'products of modernity' are alive and well, at home as much as abroad, and – courtesy of the seriously deregulated arms trade, which notoriously avoids control – permanently within reach, and carrying the risk of falling into 'the wrong hands'. Where modern industrial and organizational technologies meet timeless human enmities, explosions of violence and massive blood-letting are on the cards. The Internet delivers an opportunity for the daily, safe dress rehearsal of such explosions – grooming and honing the skills needed to set off explosions in the street. Does it also groom and hone our skills of dialogue, that *sine qua non* life-force of democracy – thereby offering a chance of arresting that de-politicization and thus de-democratization that you, with good reasons, fear?

As Richard Sennett recently suggested, a dialogue with a chance of assisting mutually beneficial cohabitation while helping to evade the pitfalls of the proximity of differences needs to be informal, open and cooperative (as opposed to contesting or combative) in disposition. Informal: entered without a predetermined agenda and procedural rules, with a hope that both will emerge in the course of the dialogue. Open: entered with a will to assume the role of learners aside that of teachers, and so to accept the possibility of being proved wrong. Cooperative: treating the dialogue as a *more-than-zero*-sum game – its purpose being not to divide the participants into winners and losers, but to allow everyone to emerge enriched in knowledge and wisdom.

Sennett's formula is everything but easy in practical application: it is not insured against mishandling, and its success is anything but guaranteed. But given the condition not of our choice, choosing that formula and trying earnestly to make it work are what, in the long run, can make all the difference between surviving together and perishing together. It is also, nevertheless, the prime vocation, duty and responsibility of all and any citizen of a democratic country.

EM 'There is no story', you write. We could stop there. There is no story, when 'After divorce, words and meaning [are] settled in two separate, incommunicado universes.' Let us try to look at the bigger picture: how could there ever be a single and autonomous story if we keep replicating the reality in our lives rather than transforming it, in a 'presentism' that narrows our horizons? The confusion between living and narrating is absolute. We live for fragments and we fragment the story; existence becomes a TV format in what you call the 'confessional society' where what matters is self-representation, regardless of the meaning of the representation, which is just an afterthought, inconsequential and even superfluous. Kurt Vonnegut wrote:

'Electronic communities build nothing. You wind up with nothing. We are dancing animals. How beautiful it is to get up and out and do something. We are here on Earth to fart around. Don't let anybody tell you any different.'[39] Maybe we are able to dance, but certainly we have forgotten how to 'get up and out and do something': we think we do not need to any more.

And here we face the final problem: this new way of living and communicating of ours, does it change the way we think? This mode of existence – in the interregnum, as we hang between the no-more and the not-yet, in an interrelation without end – is it capable of fusing our worlds together? Or of thinking our two worlds? I believe that we are becoming tributaries of the great totalizing stream. Our cultures seem to flow into the same river, reduced to affluent streams, destined to dispersion or to be thought of as tributary. Acknowledging this can help us get rid of the cultural imperialism that often makes us conceive our own partial culture – as is only natural – as universal, and makes us regard it, further, as overarching, superior, hegemonic. But it may also produce a two-dimensional conformist thought, or it may oversimplify that thought to the point of disembodying it, making it pointless to ask who we are, since the only thing that could end up mattering is where we are going.

What is certain is that, in our interconnected and reticular world, giving in to what you christen 'civic inattention' is no longer permissible. It is inconvenient, it is useless, and it is even dangerous. We must not and cannot do it any more, considering that in 2050, according to recent estimates, half the population on our continent will come from outside the EU. We must not and cannot do it anymore, because 'For the first time in history, all the peoples of the Earth have one shared present' – as Ulrich Beck put it; 'Every country has become the immediate neighbour of every other country and every man perceives the shock of events that have their epicentre on the other side of the globe.'[40] And there is a further complication: the effects of every single event, nowadays, spread according to an online process, in directions and with political and cultural consequences that are ultimately unpredictable and out of all proportion to the original event.

As you suggest, the stranger who was once so distant is now the neighbour with whom we now share our streets, public buildings, schools, workplaces. And this proximity is destabilizing, in that we do not know what to expect from the other and we are not able to remove or sidestep with one click differences that are all too real. The lost or imaginary universality of our values must give way to a challenging attempt to find our compatibility.

The risk is that this 'unity of the world' may cause a 'tremendous increase in mutual hatred and a somewhat universal irritability of everybody against everybody else', as Pankaj Mishra observes.[41] But this is not all. Europe, adds Mishra,

no longer produces, as it confidently did for two centuries, a surplus of global history; and the people that Europe used to dominate are now chafing against the norms produced by that history. The attempts to define French or European identity by violently detaching it from its presumed historic 'other', and by setting up oppositions – civilized and backward, secular and religious – cannot succeed in an age where this 'other' also possesses the power to write and make history.

But can we live two separate histories at the same time? At the same time, in the same space, right here? The Paris attacks at the hands of terroristic Islamism in 2015 immediately brought to our eyes the clash of two cultures that refuse to come together, producing a cross between anti-modernity and an evolved modernity, as Ulrich Beck called it: between the West's self-consciousness and the other's idea of the West. Once again we react, surprised by the fact that the land of democracy – the West – could ever become someone's target and enemy. More than that: that very 'someone' is a European and Western citizen just like us, and we find out that, little by little, he stripped himself of our freedom and democracy, deliberately rejecting them, only to put on a more radical culture of death. And further: we are incredulous to learn that a school in Toulouse, a Jewish museum in Brussels, a café in Sidney, the parliament in Ottawa, a kosher shop in Paris, a newspaper, a typography become targets precisely insofar as they are the stage of the grand everyday banality of our material democracy, which terroristic Islamism considers subversive; these are the normal mutual guarantees that we trade in day after day, the habitual forms and civic rules that we have given our society in our daily life, and from which we are now dying.

But here come the cartoons of *Charlie Hebdo* producing two opposite meanings, depending on the views of readers coming at them from different cultures. Those who receive and interpret the messages are not neutral subjects. The anthropologist Francesco Remotti points out that:

---

the authors and editors of the cartoons undoubtedly conjured up – explicitly or implicitly – a clearly defined 'we': a
'we' that considers it possible, legitimate, creative and funny,
to create this kind of satirical cartoons; by the same token,
they inevitably conjured up 'the other', in whose eyes these
cartoons took on a meaning that was derisive and blasphemous. In replying to such messages, those 'others' organized,
in turn, in another 'we': besides words and symbols, also
actions can mobilize the various 'we's, especially when these
are directed, collectively, destructively and with hostility,
against things or symbols that belong to 'others', or rather,
'the Other' [. . .]. But the 'we's are not always a source of
conflict and the upholders of exclusive identities. Everything
depends on how the 'we's interpret themselves and how they
envision their relation to others. It follows quite intuitively
that the more the 'we's close up on themselves and reject
otherness, the greater are the risks of conflicts and clashes.[42]

Therefore you are right in defining ours a 'superficial
multiculturalism' with a mild fascination with diversity:
'a simple flirtation with what seems exotic, in a system
that recognizes the legitimation of cultures different
from our own, but ignores or rejects all that is sacred
and non-negotiable in such cultures'.[43] The titanic task,
which is nonetheless necessary, is then that of renegotiating a new common space. The time has already come
when, as Michael Walzer puts it, 'Countries will be of
less significance to their inhabitants, because many of
these inhabitants will not have settled there that long;
the graves of their grandparents will be somewhere else;
the ground they are living on will not be regarded as
holy, and their visas will not conjur up historical and
personal memories.'[44]

And yet the Paris attacks themselves involved the misunderstanding of this kind of sacredness. In the name of the sacred image of Mohammed that had been violated, Islamist terrorists brought death into the newsroom, without realizing that it is a sacred space for Western secularism, since it sums up the autonomy from power, the right to give and receive information, and the freedom of expression and opinion. Something very peculiar happened, and it is significant that it happened in France: millions of citizens realized that freedom of expression coincides with freedom itself – it may not be of the same extent, but it is a crucial part and prerequisite of it. Therefore, it is something that belongs to us, that determines and distinguishes our culture, and for this reason it is something that we must defend. 'Freedom of speech', writes Ian McEwan,

> the giving and receiving of information, asking of awkward questions, scholarly research, criticism, fantasy, satire – the exchange within the entire range of our intellectual capacities, is the freedom that brings the others into being. Free speech is not religion's enemy, it is its protector. Because it is, there are mosques by the score in Paris, London and New York. In Riyadh, where it is absent, no churches are permitted. Importing a bible now carries the death penalty.[45]

This is far from being the cold heart of democracy, then. We could have something to believe in if only we were less cynical and more aware: if we only knew.

The only thing that is left to us is democracy, then – along with the new struggle of renegotiating every day its translation into practice, proclaiming its value as a universal method, for us, even as we know that its enemies see it as a partial ideology with a cold heart. Since we are but weak believers, unfaithful witnesses.

Democracy as the everyday habit of particular gestures, spaces, of a mutual measure, and of a balance between reality and its representation, seems to us a reduction to mediocrity, a debasement, a mere code, a sort of modern social Pi. And yet it is not a formula, but what gives shape to our shared lifestyle, what legitimizes it and allows us to exchange our freedoms, which come together and grow together so as to define a context and construct a common space.

If we lose those rules, which have become the only cultural constant of the part of the world in which we live, we are left with nothing. The ability to ask questions and the right to demand answers fail us. Public opinion gives way to common sense, which plays ball with power, because power is better than us at fabricating common sense, impersonating it and spreading it.

But now that we have reached this point, we may say that an opinion that is informed and responsible needs a functioning democracy. Not only in its rules and institutions, but also in its everyday life. What Simone Weil wrote as early as 1934 still holds: 'Never have men been so incapable, not only of subordinating their actions to their thoughts, but even of thinking.'[46] And what Albert Camus said twenty years later holds too: 'Probably it is difficult to find an epoch when the number of humiliated people was this large.'[47]

Why marvel, then, if there is no trace of a reaction, if public space is empty, if power is free from the duty to account for its own actions, which is precisely what makes Woland wonder – right before the last flight in Mikhail Bulgakov's 1966 novel *The Master and*

Margarita – whether all the scores have been settled? We are saying that there is no autonomous opinion unless the dignity of the person is safe. This is probably the Babelic puzzle of that dialectics of meaning and folly that you have described, which keeps the mystery of the future and its unpredictability wide open, no matter what. Herein lies the secret of that civic morality without which, according to Bertrand Russell, communities perish: trying to restore – again with Camus – some part of what makes up the dignity of living and dying.

We must remember that, according to the Scriptures, none other than Wisdom was attending the creation of the world; it is she who 'makes visible' knowledge and for this reason shall not 'get away from truth'. We must keep striving for wisdom, craving for understanding, committing ourselves to knowledge even when all seems lost. But then again, of course, Canetti's castigation against the failure of words and against a literature guilty of not having stopped the war, as you remind us, still holds. But this is also true about reason, it is true about beauty, it is true about technology: because it is true about man. George Steiner said that he spent his life trying to understand why art and culture never stopped inhuman acts, but rather were often their ally and ornament. Nothing guarantees or assures us of anything, since, luckily, nothing is predetermined. It depends on us: a terrible and grand statement that puts the world at stake, in the hands of man – provided that we do not forget our right and duty to ask once more today (to ask Power and ourselves) the question that Pilate pondered 2,000 years ago, when it was about the sixth hour, as he stood in front of the tripod ready to wash his hands – the West's ultimate act of cowardice –

and refused to distinguish between good and evil: *Quid est veritas?*

ZB Pontius Pilate's question acquired in recent years a second lease of life; it keeps being repeated again and again – in countless novels, plays and philosophical treatises, in the media as much as in serious conversations and idle talks. And, just as in the Gospels, with no satisfactory answer admitted thus far – which explains why that question is so much in fashion, so frequently quibbled and battled about, unlike in the not-so-distant past, when the answers, courtesy of the tough and seemingly indomitable power hierarchies, seemed obvious enough to make the question all but redundant. Today, however – as you so poignantly rub in – all sorts of different, all-too-often seemingly incompatible cultures 'seem to flow into the same river', while the era of 'cultural imperialism' is over and done with because in our multi-centred world 'the others' who hold different views on what *veritas est* 'also possess the power to write and make history'.

All those cultures engage in a furious rivalry leading all too often in practice to wars to exhaustion. As I wrote in my recent electronic conversation with Leonidas Donskis (published under the title *Liquid Evil*):

[The term 'brainwashing'] has had a spectacular career since it first appeared in print in an article published by Edward Hunter, a journalist on the *Miami News*, on 7 October 1950. The rather convoluted history of the concept to which this term refers reaches, however, deep into the Chinese tradition of Taoist teaching . . . the Taoist idea may be viewed as a case of a much wider – indeed, a well-

Interconnected loners

nigh universal – cultural phenomenon, described by Victor
Turner [48] as the 'rite of (symbolic) passage' from one social
allocation/condition to another ... Between the starting
point and the destination, there needs to be a 'transitory
stage' of a 'limbo', a 'no-man's land' – a symbolic 'social
nakedness' of sorts ... Those making the passage need first
to be bared naked – indeed, radically cleansed of the traces
of the past – in order to be admitted to their new social
identity. This is something like clearing a site for the construction of a new building – though in this case the object
of construction is the human mind-set.

I wonder whether the idea of 'brainwashing' would
be assured of such a career, exuding the same air of
veridity, indeed self-obviousness, were it to appear in
the public discourse only today – that is, seventy-odd
years later; and whether Victor Turner would proclaim
the stripped-naked mind as a universally indispensable
stage if he composed his theory of the rites of passage
in 2015, not 1969 (after all, as Hegel observed, the
metier of philosophy is weaving (conceptual) nets aimed
at 'trapping their times'). The model of 'brainwashing'
made sense in as far as it implied (indeed, presumed) the
tight coherence and implacable consistency of beliefs,
stark and unambiguous divisions between them, their
mutual exclusion and incompatibility, the impossibility
of their being held together and the virtual inconceiv-
ability of good-willed communication: all qualities that
the realities of the world split in half, and the cold war
waged between the halves separated by frontlines and
unconnected by bridges, made all but self-evident. To
be allowed to cross closely guarded borders, one needed
the quarantine of a limbo: one had first to be 'unpacked'

149

– purged, 'debriefed', stripped naked not just in the 'social' sense of nakedness. It was this mundane reality that the ideas of 'brainwashing' (when applied to a change of mind), and of 'social void' (when applied to a change of social position) were reflecting. In those realities, spiritual disengagement overlapped with territorial distantiation and estrangement, with solely the 'fifth column' daring, to their own detriment, to break the rules.

This is no longer the case because the boundaries to be crossed are nowadays notorious for their fuzziness and porousness, or because 'passages', plentiful as much as eminently reversible and so of little consequence, turned from life's milestones and points of no return into a sort of daily triviality, almost a routine – calling for no special 'rites' to be observed. No brainwashing is called for, when the brain's contents are permanently in flux and a-changing – especially among those of us, residents of the planet, who have been brought, trained and groomed to feel free, to choose free, and to act accordingly.

One consequence of elevating such freedom (bodily as much as spiritual) to the top of the value hierarchy, as we have done, is an otherwise unthinkable coexistence of oppositions (the Quran next to the Gospel and the Torah, on the same bookshelf and on the same reading list). The 'passage' between distinct identities no longer needs a limbo, a state of 'betwixt and between' to keep them apart; variation of mindset no longer demands brainwashing. People of different denominations, sometimes of starkly opposite creeds, can no longer ignore each other's real, all too real, presence, cannot fence themselves off from face-to-face encounters; and we may – needs must – cannot help but – speak to each other. We have plentiful opportunities to look at each other askance and to fight – but also a chance to talk, and so the chance to avoid shooting. Odo Marquard, a German philosopher of the neo-sceptical school – half-jokingly, but half in earnest – derives the German word for doubt (*Zweifel*) from the number two (*zwei* in German), and says the following:

> When, in relation to the sacred text, two interpreters assert, in controversy, 'I am right; my understanding of the text is the truth, and in fact – and this is necessary for salvation – in this way and not otherwise': then there can be hacking and stabbing. [. . .] Could this text not be understood, after all, in still another way, and – if that is not sufficient – still another way, and again and again in other ways?[49]

The 'pluralizing hermeneutics' that Marquard calls for, would – ought to – change a relationship dependent on 'the stubborn clinging to one's own truth' into an 'interpretive relationship'. This, according to Marquard, with whom I guess you are inclined to agree, can lead to the replacement of a 'being toward killing' with 'being toward the literary text'. And if the latter way of being prevails, there will be no room for the invocation attributed variously to Arnaud Amaury or Simone de Montfort: 'Caedite eos! Novit enim Dominus qui sunt eius' (Kill them! For the Lord knows those who are his').

A word of caution, though: as in most – perhaps all – choices you make, you gain something, you lose something else. In an enormous number of respects, debating a text is for all sides hugely advantageous over killing. But the same doubt that creates that advantage causes as well some softening – not just of tempers and manners, but of faiths. It also makes it difficult – well nigh impossible – to accept that some others may treat their own beliefs as beyond debate and therefore view us – those others' others, us who question them or refuse to treat them seriously enough – as cases of 'unwertes Leben'. It becomes well-nigh impossible to accept that there are people who are ready to murder in the name of the beliefs they hold – and to sacrifice their very life for the sake of their defence, or for the sake of manifesting that their beliefs are worth dying for. But there *are* such people, and not in a far-away, securely fenced-off land, but next door, at the next desk or on the next bench in the park. And we can't wish them away or force them to vanish.

Free people reject dogmas – and so they find dogmatism in others incomprehensible and condemnable. The contrast between 'creative and funny' and 'derisive and blasphemous', posited by Francesco Remotti whom you quote, acts both ways. A dogmatic is capable of appreciating creativity and fun in what he believes to be derisive and blasphemous no better than we, the sceptics of Marquard's ilk, are able to detect derision and blasphemy in what we know, feel, experience and practise as creative and funny.

This state of affairs no doubt presents a problem, with no short-cuts to a solution in sight. It took us millennia to put the abolition of capital punishment on the public agenda. It took us millennia to prohibit slavery. It took us millennia to promote equality of the sexes – and who would be arrogant enough to say that we have already reached all those objectives in deed, once and for all? We may hope (I do, as much as you) that our truth will eventually prevail on the planet we share, as it did (almost) in 'our' part of the globe. All the same, we need to brace ourselves for the awesome longevity of the journey, the bumpiness of the road and the limited reliability of the vehicles at our disposal. What we are confronting is what the French call *travail de longue haleine* (or, if you search for a rough English equivalent, 'a long-term and exacting job').

Be what may, I keep repeating that among the vehicles available for travelling along this road, it is a serious, good-willing dialogue (informal, open, cooperative, to quote Richard Sennett's characterization), aiming at mutual understanding and reciprocal benefit, that deserves most (even if by no means unqualified and unconditional) trust. This kind of a dialogue is not an easy or – let's admit – joyous task; it requires tough and sustained determination immune to successive – however many – adverse results, a strong sense of purpose, a great art, a readiness to admit one's own mistakes together with the arduous and toilsome duty of repairing them – and above all a lot of composure, level-headedness and patience.

Alas, the present trends do not augur well for the prospects of those requirements being promptly met. Some trends seem even to be pointing in the opposite direction. Just to pick up on one of them – all the more treacherous for the wide acclaim of its alleged benefits: a rising number of observers warn about the rising tide of 'slacktivism', aided and abetted by the rising number of websites integrating the so-called 'social sites' like Facebook or Twitter – known to allure their users to express their concerns about public issues, and their worry about the ills of society, by using their mouse to click on 'like', 'share' or 'tweet' while deluding themselves that 'they do some good without getting out of their chair'.[50] Slacktivism, a perilous stance because of its seductive promises of bodily and spiritual comfort and virtual (in more than one sense) absence of risk, may well prompt its followers to forget what the original activism was like. We are still in a quite preliminary stage of our desperate search for effective ways of recycling our intuitions into meaningful words, words into programmes, programmes into actions, and actions into realities.

The ancients used to say: *Talem habebis fructum, qualis fuerit labor* (as labour, so its fruits). It was true then. It is true still. And it will remain true for a long time to come.

Epilogue

In *No Sense of Place*, Joshua Meyrowitz points out:

> Many of the features of our 'information age' make us resemble the most primitive of social and political forms: the hunting and gathering society. As nomadic peoples, hunters and gatherers have no loyal relationship to territory. They, too, have little 'sense of place'; specific activities and behaviors are not tightly fixed to specific physical settings. The lack of boundaries both in hunting and gathering and in electronic societies leads to many striking parallels.[1]

I was very impressed when I first read this. I wondered whether this social form could also take a symbolic turn: whether it could describe the greater space of the horizons that lay down their road – since, in every age, we are at the beginning of a long journey that we have yet to make arrangements for.

So, let us wonder: how open and up for debate is the space of our horizons? The solutions offered by technology, mainstream thinking, politics' lack of autonomy, the simplification induced by high speeds are all elements of modernity that seem to push us into a big invisible funnel, in a mandatory direction, or at least a recommended one – at any rate, one with very few alternatives. In this journey, we are theoretically autonomous; we would like to be free. We may refuse. We may slow down or march on. We may not be a part of the track, but make use of it without being passive. If we are equipped with the weapon of doubting, we may manage the seductiveness that accompanies the manifest benefits of modernity; faced with each innovative solution, we may ask: who leads this process? And, as for me, am I a user of the system in which I move or am I being used? What actual freedom is there in the purported choice that I seem to have just made?

There was a time when, in some regimes, the autonomy of the individual had to be upheld against the pervasive totality of the system that cancelled them. Today, we must give the right value to the solitude of the individual – make sure it is an intelligent, conscious solitude: in this case too, an autonomous solitude, even though by the opposite process. Maintaining one's ability to choose means leaving different options open – that is, leaving the space for action, for political action. The problem almost seems physical, but it is actually cultural. It may be worth finding inspiration in a crucial passage of *The Master and Margarita*, a book that, during the Soviet dictatorship, was read in Russia as a prophecy, in spite of everything around it – in spite of the weight of reality, the power balance, the rule of a kind of power that was engineered to resist through all eternity: 'Something will happen, because a situation like this can't drag on forever.'[2]

This quote from Bulgakov is enough to open up the

horizons. Indeed, Margarita 'had dreamed of a place, mournful, desolate, under a dull sky of early spring. The sky was leaden, with tufts of low, scudding grey clouds and filled with a numberless flock of rooks.' Suddenly, the door of a log cabin is flung open and 'he appeared', at a fair distance, with ruffled hair, unshaven. He waves and calls her. 'Panting in the lifeless air, Margarita started running towards him over the uneven, tussocky ground. At that moment she woke up.' ' "I believe it!", whispered Margarita solemnly. "I believe something is going to happen."' After a while, she starts flying over an expanse of roofs, a sea of shimmering electric lights, 'alone with the moon, sailing along above her and to the left'. Unbelievably, everything is still possible.

In the moment of his utmost desperation, when he realizes that he cannot publish *The Master* and he entrusts it to his wife so that she may keep it safe in the wardrobe where his 'assassinated plays' lie hidden, Bulgakov seems to repeat to himself the same formula: 'At any rate, we do not know the future that awaits us.'

This space that we hold on to, still unknown, still open to debate, is the road out of Babel.

The horizons are open.

Ezio Mauro

Notes

Prologue

1 Quoted in Andrew Hurley's translation – see Borges, *Collected Fictions* (London, 1999), pp. 101–6.
2 Alan Turing, 'Computing machinery and intelligence', *Mind*, 69 (1950).

1 Inside a dematerialized space

1 Thomas Paine, *Common Sense* [1776] (London, 2004), p. 5.
2 Thomas Hobbes, *Leviathan* [1651] I, xiii, 9 (Oxford, 2008), p. 76.
3 J. M. Coetzee, *Diary of a Bad Year* (London, 2007), pp. 8, 12.
4 José Saramago, *Ensaio sobre a lucidez* [2004] (English trans. *Seeing* (London, 2006)).
5 Walter Lippmann, *The Phantom Public: A Sequel to Public Opinion* (New York, 1925), p. 13.
6 Jacques Julliard, *La reine du monde: essai sur la démocratie d'opinion* (Paris, 2008).
7 Benjamin Barber, *If Mayors Ruled the World:*

Dysfunctional Nations, Rising Cities (New Haven, 2013), pp. 3, 76–7.

8 Friedrich Nietzsche, *Götzen-Dämmerung: Oder wie Man mit dem Hammer philosophirt* [1889] (English trans. in *The Anti-Christ, Ecce Homo, Twilight of the Idols and other Writings* (Cambridge, 2005), p. 209).

9 Slavoj Žižek, *Demanding the Impossible* (Cambridge, 2013), p. 39.

10 Barber, *If Mayors Ruled the World*, pp. 3, 4. The provoking title is complemented by its yet more inspiring and incensing subtitle: 'Dysfunctional nations, rising cities'.

11 Joke Brouwer and Sjoerd van Tuinen (eds.), *Giving and Taking: Antidotes to a Culture of Greed* (Rotterdam, 2014), p. 5. Although Brouwer and van Tuinen's statement in the preface to the book they edit is perhaps slightly too optimistic, their observation should not be overlooked.

12 See the interview on giving and taking included in *ibid.*, pp. 10–11.

13 Arlie Russell Hochschild, *The Outsourced Self: What Happens When We Pay Others to Live Our Lives For Us* (New York, 2012), p. 8.

14 Jeremy Rifkin, *The Zero Marginal Cost Society* (New York, 2014), pp. 121, 125, 132.

15 Ulrich Beck, *Was ist Globalisierung?* [1997] (English trans. *What is Globalization?* (Cambridge, 2000), p. 62).

16 Jürgen Habermas, *Legitimationsprobleme im Spätkapitalismus* [1973] (English trans. *Legitimation Crisis* (London, 1976)).

17 Peter Sloterdijk, 'What does a human have that he

can give away?' in Brouwer and van Tuinen (eds.), *Giving and Taking*, pp. 16–17.

18 Coetzee, *Diary of a Bad Year*, pp. 77, 119.

2 Inside a changing social space

1 Vladimir Jankélévitch, *Le je-ne-sais-quoi et le presque-rien*, vol. II: *La méconnaissance, le malentendu* (Paris, 1957).

2 Hans Fallada, *Jeder stirbt für sich allein* [1947] (English trans. *Every Man Dies Alone* (New York, 2009)).

3 Albert Camus, *L'homme révolté* [1951] (English trans. *The Rebel* (London, 1953), p. 26).

4 Thomas Piketty, *Le capital au XXI siècle* [2013] (English trans. *Capital in the Twenty-first Century* (Cambridge, Mass., 2014), p. 1).

5 Hans-Georg Gadamer, *Wahrheit und Methode: Grundzüge einer philosophischen Hermeneutik* [1960] (English trans. *Truth and Method* (2nd revised edition) (New York, 2000), p. 397).

6 John Kenneth Galbraith, *The Affluent Society* (New York, 1958), p. 352.

7 Alain Touraine, interviewed in *La Repubblica* (3 October 2014).

8 See Enrico Deaglio in *La Repubblica* (5 October 2014).

9 Tony Judt, *Ill Fares the Land* (London, 2010), p. 34.

10 José Saramago, *O caderno* [2009] (English trans. *The Notebook* (London, 2010), pp. 67, 27, 19, 18).

11 Paul Auster and J. M. Coetzee, *Here and Now, Letters 2008–2011* (New York, 2014), pp. 20–1.

12 Antonio Gramsci, *Lettere dal carcere* [1948] (English trans. *Letters from Prison* (New York, 1994), I,

p. 299 (from a letter to his brother Carlo on 19 December 1929), and pp. 330–1 (to his sister-in-law Tatiana)).

13 Antonio Gramsci, *Quaderni dal carcere* (Turin, 1971).

14 Ivan Krastev, 'From politics to protest', in *Journal of Democracy*, 25 (October 2014), 4, pp. 5–19, p. 10.

15 *Ibid.*, p. 11.

16 *Ibid.*, pp. 13–14.

17 Neil Postman, *Amusing Ourselves to Death* (London, 1985), p. 4.

18 *Ibid.*, pp. 155–6.

19 Walter Lippmann, *Public Opinion* [1922] (Mineola, NY, 2004), pp. 15–16.

20 See, for instance, http://home.comcast.net/~lionelin gram/The%20Benefits%20of%20Soft%20Power. pdf.

21 Michel Serres, *Petite Poucette* [2012] (English trans. *Thumbelina: The Culture and Technology of Millennials* (Lanham, Md, 2015); this and the following quotations are at pp. 7, 63, 10, 6, 9–10, respectively).

3 Interconnected loners

1 Manuel Castells, *Communication Power* (Oxford, 2013), p. 55.

2 *Ibid.*, p. 58.

3 *Ibid.*, p. 50.

4 *Ibid.*, p. 35.

5 Zygmunt Bauman and David Lyon, *Liquid Surveillance* (Cambridge, 2013).

6 Nicholas Negroponte, interviewed by Riccardo Staglianò in *La Repubblica* (30 November 2014).

7 William Carlos Williams, *In the American Grain* (New York, 1925), p. i.

8 Neil Postman, *Amusing Ourselves to Death* (London, 1985), p. 44.

9 Bertrand Russell, *Power* [1938] (London, 2004), p. 247.

10 Todd Gitlin, *The Whole World is Watching: Mass Media in the Making and Unmaking of the New Left* (Berkeley, Los Angeles, 1980), p. 28.

11 See Kendra Cherry, 'The Milgram obedience experiment' (2008), retrieved from http://psychology.about.com/od/socialinfluence/fl/What-Is-Obedience.htm.

12 See www.ted.com/talks/philip_zimbardo_on_the_psychology_of_evil.

13 See Christopher Browning, *Ordinary Men: Reserve Police Battalion 101 and the Final Solution in Poland* (New York, 1992).

14 See http://en.wikipedia.org/wiki/The_Blair_Witch_Project#Plot.

15 Clay Shirky, *Here Comes Everybody: The Power of Organizing Without Organizations* (London, 2008), p. 55. The following quotations are at pp. 77, 55, 57, 58, 66, 98, 81.

16 Walter Lippmann, *Public Opinion* [1922] (Mineola, NY, 2004), pp. 28–9.

17 Shirky, *Here Comes Everybody*, p. 17.

18 Tony Judt, *Ill Fares the Land* (London, 2010), p. 120.

19 Castells, *Communication Power*, pp. 117, 15.

20 Werner Herzog, interviewed by Dario Olivero in *La Repubblica* (13 November 2014).

21 See Georg Simmel, 'Metropolis and mental life', in

Classic Essays on the Culture of Cities, ed. Richard Sennett (New York, 1969), pp. 47–60 (reprint of Kurt Wolff's translation (New York, 1950)).

22 'On the tram', as translated by Willa Muir and Edwin Muir and published in *The Collected Short Stories of Franz Kafka* (London, 1988), p. 388.

23 'The new advocate', in *The Collected Short Stories of Franz Kafka*, p. 415.

24 Lippmann, *Public Opinion*, p. 130.

25 Negroponte, in the interview quoted in n.6 above.

26 Michel Foucault, 'The order of discourse' [1970], in *Untying the Text: A Post-structuralist Reader*, ed. Robert Young (London, 1981), p. 67.

27 Andre Geim, interviewed by Enrico Franceschini in *La Repubblica* (4 January 2015).

28 Walter Benjamin, *Schriften* [1955] (English trans. 'The work of art in the age of mechanical reproduction', in *Illuminations* (London, 1999), p. 216).

29 Castells, *Communication Power*, pp. 137, 144, 145.

30 Gustave Le Bon, *Psychologies des foules* [1895] (English trans. *The Crowd: A Study of the Popular Mind* (New York, 1986), pp. 2, 19–20, 49, 56, 60–1).

31 Evgeny Morozov, *The Net Delusion: How Not to Liberate the World* (London, 2011), pp. 20, 31, 218, 59.

32 Ivor Richards and Cecyl Ogden, *The Meaning of Meaning: A Study of the Influence of Language upon Thought and of the Science of Symbolism* (New York, 1923), p. 1.

33 Bronisław Malinowski, 'The problem of meaning in primitive languages', in *ibid.*, p. 316.

34 www.economist.com/node/17848401.

---

35 See Pat Kane's review of Evgeny Morozov's *The Net Delusion* in the *Independent* (7 January 2012).
36 See his review of the above book in the *Guardian*: www.guardian.co.uk/technology/2011/jan/13/evg eny-morozov-the-net-delusion.
37 Under the title *The Net Delusion: How Not to Liberate the World* (London, 2012). The American version, published by Public Affairs, bears the title *The Net Delusion: The Dark Side of Internet Freedom*.
38 See Bauman and Lyon, *Liquid Surveillance*.
39 Kurt Vonnegut, *A Man Without a Country* (New York, 2005), p. 62.
40 Ulrich Beck in *La Repubblica* (1 November 2006).
41 Pankaj Mishra in *La Repubblica* (8 February 2015).
42 Francesco Remotti, *Cultura: dalla complessità all'impoverimento* (Rome, 2011), p. 116.
43 Zygmunt Bauman, interviewed by Natale Maria Serena in *Il Corriere della Sera* (12 January 2015).
44 Michael Walzer in *La Repubblica* (8 February 2015).
45 Ian McEwan, 'Not religion's enemy but its protector', retrieved from www.eurozine.com/articles/2015-03-11-mcewan-en.html.
46 Simone Weil, *Waiting on Truth* (Oxford, 1988).
47 Albert Camus, *L'avenir de la civilisation européenne: entretien avec Albert Camus* (Athens, 1956).
48 See his *The Ritual Process: Structure and Anti-Structure* (Chicago, 1969), p. 97.
49 Odo Marquard, *Farewell to Matters of Principle: Philosophical Studies* (Oxford, 1989), p. 123.
50 See Barnaby Feder's article 'They weren't careful what they hoped for', in the *New York Times*, retrieved from www.nytimes.com/2002/05/29/nyregion/they-weren-t-careful-what-they-hoped-for.html.

Epilogue
1 Joshua Meyrowitz, *No Sense of Place: The Impact of Electronic Media on Social Behavior* (New York, 1985), p. 315.
2 Mikhail Bulgakov, *Мастер и Маргарита* [1966–7] (English trans. *The Master and Margarita* (London, 2003)), pp. 251–2.